"Live Humbly, Serve Graciously" is a timeless book. The call to action throughout is supported by the personalization of the text, scripture references, and prayers. Each reflection enlightened, empowered, and educated me. I sensed this is the book that Jeff has been waiting to write all of his life. It is a blessing that should be shared.

LaRhonda Julien

Sometimes we come away from retreats feeling holier than when we arrived and have genuine plans to continue our spiritual growth. But then we return to the real world and so often lose our resolve. "Live Humbly, Serve Graciously" is like 24 (25 with the epilogue) gift cards to fine restaurants that will help me stay spiritually fed throughout the year so I don't lose my resolve. I am looking forward to having this book with me during my regular weekly hour of adoration. Thank you for this gift!

Bob Chapin
Senior Vice-President, CharterBank

Jeff Armbruster has done it again! In "Live Humbly, Serve Graciously" he challenges us to hold true to our baptismal promises and expectations. Jeff weaves together biblical references, stories of the saints, and personal anecdotes to present a bold and heartfelt roadmap to becoming a better Christian. It's a game changer and a must read for those of us looking to form a closer bond with Christ.

David McCullough
Vice President, eBureau

It is said that Jesus's words in Matthew telling us to love God and also love others are at the "heart of Christian instruction." In Jeff's 24 reflections he tells us how humility and service can bring that instruction into the real world and our personal lives. Lists of actions we can take and a multitude of inspirational references guarantee the reader will grow personally and spiritually. "Live Humbly, Serve Graciously" is a learning opportunity both for Catholics and non-Catholics alike.

Fred Weil
President, Image Group of Georgia

In Jeff Armbruster's newest book, "Live Humbly, Serve Graciously: Reflections on Baptism, Mission and Service," he takes the reader along with him on his own personal journey of Christian mission and service as he combs through scripture to support his experience. With a vulnerability reminiscent of Thomas Merton, he is also able to courageously and authentically share his own inner struggles in regard to fully becoming the Christian that he knows God has called him to be. Anyone who is serious about their ongoing conversion while continuing to serve others more authentically, will want to read and re-read this book.

Michael B. Vaissade
R.N., B.A. Theology

Many of us live our lives in a distracted state where we are often preoccupied by life's daily demands. "Live, Humbly, Serve Graciously" reminds us, and invites us, to find sacred footing in our busy lives. No matter where you are, or what you are doing, you will find that these reflections will not only nurture your soul, but they will also inspire you to embrace humility, service and love – the simple graces that enrich our lives.

Margaret A. Piekarski

I have been blessed to hear Jeff Armbruster deliver many of his reflections in our men's fellowship group at Mary Our Queen Catholic Church. Through these reflections, and in personal conversation, Jeff has been a guiding and calming influence in both my spiritual and professional life. He has received the spiritual gifts of leadership, service and humility and constantly reminds me that you cannot demonstrate one without the others. It was with excitement then, that I was given an opportunity to review, "Live Humbly, Serve Graciously." Having done so, I am certain that the reader will find the same calming and rewarding effects. You will turn these pages with a warm smile on your face.

David Hancharik
Technical Director, ViaSat, Inc.

Jeff has the gift of being able to present a wide range of spiritual and non-spiritual life topics in a concise accessible manner. Any one of these topics could easily warrant volumes, but Jeff's writing invites the reader into his mind and heart for just long enough to evoke a conversation in the reader's own mind. I find myself using Jeff's books as tools that I pick up and put down many times, taking what I need (or may not have known that I need) at a particular moment and then contemplating the meaning of his experiences and messages in my own life. And, knowing Jeff, this is by design, although perhaps not his, but His.

Chris Dillon
Partner, Jones Day

I am grateful to be asked to read this book by Jeff Armbruster, a student of mine 52 years ago. It's beautifully written and conveys a deep spirituality. The concept of "aggressive humility" (epilogue) is a new and powerful insight into how to live our lives as baptized Christians. I highly recommend this book.

Sr. Louise Marie Willenbrink, OSU

Some books leave a mark and inspire you to do more with your life. "Live Humbly, Serve Graciously: Reflections on Baptism, Mission and Service" by Jeff Armbruster is one such book. Jeff's compelling journey as a Catholic man, husband, father and business leader is a faith-filled adventure that makes us draw closer to Christ and enthusiastically embrace the mission He has in store for us in our own lives. I strongly recommend Jeff's excellent work and hope it is widely read by anyone not satisfied with an ordinary life.

Randy Hain
President, Serviam Partners
Author of "Journey to Heaven: A Roadmap for Catholic Men";
"The Catholic Briefcase: Tools for Integrating Faith and Work";
and "Joyful Witness: How to be an Extraordinary Catholic"

Jeff Armbruster's, "Live Humbly, Serve Graciously" is a collection of two dozen thought-provoking reflections, heavily influenced by Blessed John Henry Cardinal Newman's prayer, "The Mission of My Life." The reflections provide a wonderful foundation for anyone with a desire to grow more deeply in their interior life. I highly recommend this book as an excellent means of evaluating one's own spiritual journey by examining how we are living our God-given vocations through prayer, service, love and humility.

Deacon James E. Stone,
Director of Religious Education
Mary Our Queen Catholic Church
Peachtree Corners, Georgia.

The greatest of all truths is simply that God is. He exists! Another great truth is that from His infinite goodness, He created each of us to share in His goodness and beatitude. Made in His image, we are all here in this earthly life as pilgrims who journey to the heavenly shores of eternity. We are neither accidents of nature nor gods of our own making. God made us, loves us and calls us to share in His holy life. Jeff Armbruster has captured these foundational truths in his new book, "Live Humbly, Serve Graciously." I strongly recommend it to aid you in your spiritual life and mission in this world.

All of us question the meaning of life, wanting to know who and why we are. Too many of us have either forgotten or have never been told of our noble purpose. Jeff recognized and was reminded of his purpose in the prayer of Blessed John Henry Newman, The Mission of my Life, "God has created me to do Him some definite service...I have my mission..."

Jeff has created a series of reflections that help us navigate the path to Heaven that begins with baptism into God's family and culminates in the arms of our Merciful Father and the Beatific Vision. Focused on the person of Our Lord and Savior, Jesus Christ, and enriched immeasurably with God's Holy Word, Jeff offers us examples from his own walk in faith that are both moving and a blessing. They will help you along your own spiritual journey, loving God, serving those He places in your life, and discovering your own particular mission in the ordinary moments of your life.

Deacon Mike Bickerstaff
Director of Adult Education,
St. Peter Chanel Catholic Church, Roswell, Georgia;
Editor-in-Chief, Integrated Catholic Life, Inc.

Live Humbly, Serve Graciously

Reflections on Baptism, Mission and Service

Jeffrey T. Armbruster

Foreword by Rev. Lawrence J. McNeil

To Jim

God has created you to do the definite service. Some definite service you have your mission!

God bless you

Jeff

First printing October 2016

IBSN 9781536871845

Note:
Throughout this book, all passages from Sacred Scripture were taken from the New American Bible, Revised Edition (NABRE), and downloaded from the U.S. Conference of Catholic Bishops website, usccb.org.

Cover design and photography by Patti Armbruster

Printed by CreateSpace

Dedication

This book is dedicated to my wife, Laurel;
to our children and their spouses,
Amy and Dan, Dave and Patti;
to our grandchildren Zach, Ellie and Nick,
and any others we may be blessed with;
to our many relatives and friends;
to the priests and religious who have
touched my life so significantly;
and to each of you who choose to read
even a small portion of this work.

My fondest hope is that in some way you will be touched
by the Holy Spirit and be inspired to live humble lives by
graciously serving everyone you encounter
along life's journey.

God bless each of you,
you are truly special gifts from God.

Contents

Acknowledgments

Should you choose to take your valuable time to read the pages that follow, please understand that most of what you encounter is the result of what I have learned from many others and represents the gifts they have generously shared or given me.

At the top of the list of those from whom I have learned much and to whom I am eternally grateful and owe much is, Laurel, my wife of forty-seven years. She has endured much during that time, including addresses in six different states during our first twelve years of marriage as I pursued my career. Laurel has loved me unconditionally, taught me much, and challenged me often. Her insights are remarkable. She lifts me up when I am down, and brings me back to earth when I fly off on a tangent. She continues to give me gifts beyond what I deserve by simultaneously being my strongest supporter, most severe critic and best friend. She makes me be a better person. Most important, though, she has been my spiritual partner and soul mate throughout our lives together. We have grown together spiritually in ways I could never have foreseen, in our prayer life, in raising our family, in how we live our lives. Her love of God, trust in Jesus Christ for all things, and openness to the Holy Spirit's guidance constantly force me to up my game. My love for the Lord has been so very profoundly influence by her. She truly lives her life devoted to getting herself, me, our children and their families, and our extended families and friends to heaven and devotes much spiritual, emotional, mental and physical energy to that commitment. I am indeed blessed to have this woman walking hand-in-hand with me through life.

Our children, Amy and David, and their spouses Dan and Patti provide incredible support and encouragement as do

i

our grandchildren, Zach, Ellie and Nicholas. Life is so much fuller because of each them, their joy and spirit. We have been eternally blessed because of them.

My parents, Frank and Jane Armbruster, provided not only a firm foundation for life, particularly by the admirable way they lived their lives, they also provided lifelong encouragement to me and my siblings to grow and give. My faith foundation was firmly established under their guidance. How could they ever be adequately thanked for setting that firm base? The manner in which my sister Becky practices her faith, too, is an inspiration.

There are so many other family members (both outlaws and in-laws) who have given me so much through their (and our) life experiences that trying to name them all would surely result in forgetting some. However, my sister-in-law Junie Brown does deserve special mention because she plowed through my manuscript, edited it thoroughly and challenged me to reach deeper and express my ideas clearer. I owe her a huge thank you.

I am most grateful to my daughter-in-law Patti Armbruster for applying her artistic talents to the design and creation of the cover and interior of this book. The design is based on her interpretation of several key messages contained in this book — specifically that as Christians, as Catholics, our job in this life is to live humbly and serve graciously no matter where we are, who we are with and what the situation might be. Doing so can only be done when we model our lives after Jesus, who demonstrated throughout His life just what it means to live humbly no matter what and to graciously serve others unconditionally, even if it means giving our life for another. Thank you Patti, you are special.

In addition, there are many, many friends who have loved and taught me much though their generosity and experiences. One of those dear friends, Father Larry McNeil, has had a huge impact on my life in so many ways. His unconditional love and support for more than forty years has been such a blessing. Thanks to the Holy Spirit for nudging me to sit and talk with him those many years ago, when my courage to do so was lacking. The spiritual and emotional support he has provided me and our family has been a true gift. To him I will always be thankful. The words of the foreword to this book are lovingly and gratefully acknowledged – what a blessing to work with him on this project.

But throughout my life I have been blessed to have crossed paths with so many others who have significantly impacted my life spiritually and otherwise. The wonderful nuns and lay teachers, at four different Catholic parochial schools I attended from kindergarten through high school, not only taught me but they also dedicated themselves to showing the beauty of Jesus' love and service to me. To the dozens of priests at the many parishes I have been a member of throughout my lifetime, each, in some way helped me grow and mature in my spiritual journey. Even decades later, I clearly recall vitally important messages (eternal-life-messages) from memorable homilies, conversations and instruction. While there are many, I would particularly like to thank Fathers Ed Everitt, Stephen Hribick, Sylvan Capitani, Herald Broch, John Anthony, Tim Gadziala, Richard Lopez, Dan Ketter, Miguel Grave de Peralta and David Dye. Each of these devoted servants of Christ have touch my life profoundly and to each I am genuinely grateful.

Several ordained deacons have also challenged me to develop in ways I would not have otherwise done, most notably, my dear friend Deacon Jim Stone. Over the past several years he has challenged me (nearly) daily to seek a deeper relationship with the Father, Son and Holy Spirit through prayer and other devotions, he openly shares himself with love and vulnerability, and provides encouragement when needed. Several years ago I was blessed to share the presentation of a three-day Lenten mission at our parish with

Jim and cannot describe the benefits I received from that collaboration.

Many friends and colleagues over the years have also, each in their own way, showed me the joy of work and friendship and what it means to do everything with love. They put up with my pride, arrogance and other warts, yet they loved me just the same. Many of my bosses over the years also taught me the value of recognizing the talents in others, and without saying so specifically, taught me how to help others grow to their full potential. They taught me, too, again without saying so specifically, the importance of being a link in a chain of relationships. Many of them gave me chances that did not seem reasonable, and challenged me to reach deep, grow and perform. To them all, thank you sincerely.

As a consultant for the past fourteen years, I have crossed paths with many clients who have allowed me to share my faith with them. Quite surprising how frequently clients have asked how to handle a work challenge, and after much conversation they realized for themselves their answer nearly always has a spiritual foundation. Living humbly and serving others graciously transcends all parts of our lives. Some genuinely joyful "ah-ha" moments have been shared over the years.

And I could not complete these acknowledgements without thanking the remarkable group of guys I have been meeting with at Mary Our Queen parish, nearly every Friday morning at 6:30 a.m. for about a dozen years. Early versions of most of the material contained in this volume were compiled, massaged, and shared with them as part of our round-robin sharing of "speaker" duties within the group. They have been extremely supportive and tolerant as I shared my thoughts and feelings on a wide range of spiritual topics. Hopefully we have all grown together in our love of Jesus, and will continue to do so moving forward. They have been an important part of my spiritual journey for more than a decade.

And finally, I am grateful to the many with whom I share my faith. I have prayed with them and for them and they have prayed for me and my family. Many of the insights shared here come from them. They are each a blessing!

Foreword

On October 2, 2006, Charles Roberts, IV approached an Old Order Amish school house in Nickel Mines, PA, expelled the adults and boys, tied up ten girls, ages 6 – 13, and shot them, killing 5, before he committed suicide. As the Amish community gathered, their response many around the world found more shocking than the horrid crime. One grandfather warned young relatives not to think evil of this man, and another father reminded others that "he had a mother and wife and a soul" and now was standing before a just God. Members of the community that day visited the murderer's family and spent time comforting them. Members of the Amish community attended Roberts' funeral, and they also set up a charitable fund for the family of the shooter. For them, Justice was in God's hands and we need only live the Gospel of peace and forgiveness. What kind of strange people are these not to want vengeance?

As I read through Jeff Armbruster's book, *Live Humbly, Serve Graciously: Reflections on Baptism, Mission and Service,* this story came to mind again and again, because these Amish were baptized Christians, and they responded out of the Gospel that was the core of their lives and their actions. They come from an ancient Christian reality that amazed the Romans who, even as they persecuted Christians marveled – see how these Christians love one another!

I've known Jeff and Laurel for all but 40 years, and have come to know them and their family as true Christians, Catholics who strive to live their faith. And that is what this book is about – living the Gospel as Christian and specifically

Catholic believers. And it is written by a man who is no religious fanatic or even a professional preacher. Jeff is a scientist, who worked for decades in the US Geological Survey. He is a noted speaker and facilitator in the areas of principle centered leadership and has been a sought out guide in leadership and mentoring by both governmental and private sectors. He is a wise mentor, an engaging speaker, a wonderful exemplar of the leadership skills he seeks to share. His first book, *Some Practical Lessons in Leadership*, is an excellent collection of the most practical lessons in true leadership culled from his decades of listening, learning, serving and leading. I've worked beside Jeff, and seen his effect and affect on people. He lives what he teaches.

But this book is different from the first book. It isn't about lessons to be learned, but rather reflections to be shared and mulled over. While it is informed by his life experiences it is rooted in his faith. It is written by a believer who has decided to share the heart of his life – a loving God who has filled us with life from the first moment of conception. It is about the Mystery of sacrifice and service; the power of humility and love.

Jeff is convinced that God exists, that He is central to the understanding of life, and that the relationship between a person and God must be intimate and real and powerful if the person is to make any sense out of life. God does not inhibit him or narrow him, rather God and faith invigorate him and allow him to use all his abilities to their fullest potential. Throughout his life and work he has never forced his faith upon anyone, but anyone who has worked with him has known from the first that he was and is a man of faith – and in that he follows in the footsteps of such folk as Gregor Mendel, Marie Cure, Louis Pasteur, Albert Einstein to name a few.

This book is not about confrontation between religious folk and secularists, it is rather an invitation from one

Catholic to his fellow Catholics (and by extension other Christians and men and women of faith) to rediscover their faith and to live it daily. We speak of practicing our faith – much as a musician or doctor or athlete or lawyer practices – precisely because if it isn't done daily it gradually fades away. As he quotes the Dalai Lama: "Put pursuit of virtue at the heart of daily life".

And at the start of the book Jeff introduces us to John Cardinal Newman's prayer entitled, *The Mission of My Life*. And I believe he allows that prayer to become the guide throughout the book.

He speaks of pride and humility and shares his belief that they are at the heart of the struggle to be human and to be holy. We are to serve – as the old *Baltimore Catholic Catechism* would say: "Why did God make me? He made me to know Him, to love Him and to serve Him in this life and to be happy with Him forever in heaven." He proclaims that Baptism is the start of our journey, and we must embrace it and live it if we are to understand that which makes us happy, and makes us fully human.

Baptism is not just received, it must be lived out. And for Jeff (and for the Church) that means that our love for God touches all aspects of life and our faith must permeate everything we do. And here in this book he invites us to ask a most important question, is our faith part of every decision and action of our lives or is it something we keep hidden? Perhaps I might state it a bit differently – are we Catholics who happen to be Americans or Americans who happen to be Catholic?

Jeff shows us that everything in life is permeated by God, and it is impossible to read scripture or believe in God and not believe in moral absolutes.

He reminds us that if we are going to be people of faith then we must make the Eucharist and prayer and reconciliation be central to our lives. These are the tools, along with the grace of Baptism, that will enable us to confront sin and selfishness and pride in our lives and stand up for what we believe. Every reflection again and again challenges us to see the struggle as real. He speaks of practical, everyday ways to implement faith in our lives, to live out what we believe, and to take our right to speak our minds in the public square seriously.

And thus while you read this book sometimes you might find yourself nodding in agreement, and at other times bridling at a strident challenge to your opinion, but the book is never anything less than honest, open and heartfelt, and always springs from Jeff's faith and conviction. Whether he is talking about battling Goliath or foot washing, abortion or missionary service, Jeff is sharing himself. I found myself constantly distracted as I read, looking from the text into my own life and how I take to heart Jeff's message. In many ways it is a great book for spiritual reading, all the more powerful because it is not reflections based on theology and philosophy but on the life of Jeff Armbruster.

It is a simple yet powerful book – after all, who would reflect on the laughter of Abraham and Sarah at the announcement of the birth of their son and suggest that Isaac in English should be translated LOL. He invites us to reflect on the role of thankfulness in our lives, and the humility that empowers us as it did the Blessed Virgin Mary. He offers practical steps, interwoven with Scripture and quotes from a wide range of wise men and women, that will help us to move beyond simply believing to practicing our faith – and that brings me back to those Amish men and women in Nickel Mines who did not simply believe in God, but walked daily with Him.

And maybe after all that is exactly what this book is all about, living out what Micah had to say:

"You have been told, O Man, what is good, and what the Lord requires of you; Only to do right, and to love goodness and to walk humbly with your God."
Micah (6:8)

Rev. Lawrence J. McNeil, D.Min.
Retired Pastor
Basilica of the Sacred Heart of Jesus
Hanover, PA
Adjunct Professor
Mount Saint Mary's Seminary
Emmitsburg, MD

Prologue – The Mission of My Life

Roughly 55 years ago, a skinny little guy, barely 5 feet tall and less than 90 pounds began his (my) high school career at the newly established Cardinal Newman High School in Columbia, South Carolina. About three months into my freshman year we moved from the old Ursuline Convent in downtown Columbia into our brand new building on the north side of town. My class would become the first class to graduate after attending all four years in the new school.

Fast forward fifty years, to May, 2014, and I found myself sitting with my wife, Laurel, and several of my classmates, at the graduation ceremony of my school to be awarded a 50-year golden anniversary diploma. The school chaplain, Father Andrew Trapp, opened the ceremony with a prayer. Even though I had attended the school for four years, and knew a good deal about our patron, Blessed John Henry Cardinal Newman, I had never heard the prayer written by him which Father Trapp read aloud that day. I was spellbound by the words of this beautiful prayer and knew at that moment something profound had touched my heart.

Over the past year or so I have spent many hours reflecting quietly on the meaning and power of Cardinal Newman's prayer, particularly as it applies to my own life, the roles that God has given me to fulfill, the importance of the part I must play in the lives of my wife, children and grandchildren, the impact on them should I fail to faithfully carry out what God intends for me to do as part of His marvelous and intricately complex grand plan, and the spill over effects of my decisions and actions on every person I come in contact with over my lifetime.

For the past twelve years or so, I have met with a dozen (plus or minus) men from my Church at 6:30 a.m. every Friday morning. Our Men's Spiritual Fellowship gatherings consist of a half-hour talk by one of the members (we rotate speaking assignments), followed by attending 7:00 a.m. Mass, and concluding by further reflecting on the talk given that morning over coffee. On about a 3-month rotation, the responsibility for the presentation is mine, so I have written quite a few talks over the time we have been meeting.

As a result of my reflection on Cardinal Newman's prayer, *The Mission of My Life*, I became aware that many of the talks I have given over the past decade, just happen to have been related to the message of that prayer, specifically, that God has a plan for each of us (me), that His plan includes an initiation we Christians call Baptism, that there are obligations and responsibilities that go along with the gift of Baptism, and that we are all on a life-long journey to learn how to serve others as Jesus taught and modeled for us. If we choose to faithfully live out God's plan for us, we will enjoy eternity with Him.

This book is my way of sharing many of the thoughts and feelings surrounding these topics, all related to the mission of my life, in hopes that you may be touched in some positive way to initiate, or renew your resolve to live a life of service to others, and by serving others you will be filled with the joy that comes from serving God. Each reflection was inspired by a homily, a scripture passage, a prayer from the *Book of Christian Prayer (Liturgy of the Hours)*, a meditation from *The Word Among Us* (a Catholic periodical), or some other book or person I was blessed to intersect with. You will discover that several of the reflections were inspired by current events and political discourse (even though events have transpired beyond those described) and in a couple of cases a life situation directly involving my family and me. Several reflections are heavily based on a thought or theme that I wrote about in my first book, *Some Practical Lessons in Leadership – Observations from Daily Life*, but with new insights beyond those in the original writing.

Each copy of that first book I have signed includes the invitation to "Lead Humbly and Serve Graciously." As I struggled with naming this work, I ran across a printed version of that inscription, and realized that "Live Humbly, Serve Graciously" is what it means to live out our responsibilities as Catholics, as Christians. My reflections on the power of humble living and gracious service are profoundly linked to the ideas in the final chapter of the earlier work entitled "The Power of Leading with Aggressive Humility." In a very real sense, that reflection could actually be rewritten by simply doing a search and replace of 'lead' or 'leadership' with 'life' or 'living.'

As I began studying the twenty five or so individual compositions directly related to baptism, mission and service, I was quite confident that I would be able to arrange them neatly in some reasonable order based on those three topics. I discovered, however, that these three topics are so intricately interwoven, I could not neatly separate them into these three categories. For example, my reflections on baptism, particularly those related to my obligation to be priest, prophet and king, could not be separated from those about my responsibility to be a servant leader. Further, I discovered that my baptismal obligations and my responsibility to serve others constitute the fundamental definition of what it means for me to dedicate my life to living the mission for which God created me. As much as I tried to find a logical sequence, that order simply did not reveal itself. In my earlier book, I chose to present the leadership observations in the order in which I had written them because each stood nearly independently of the others. With the reflections that constitute this current effort, while I have tried to present them in what seems to me to be a logical order based on their content, almost surely you, the reader and my companion on life's journey, will find more logical ways to order them. For the most part they can be read in any order that makes sense to you. And while this work is heavily slanted toward those who are Catholic Christians, I believe Christians of all faith traditions will find the thoughts and challenges here to be useful.

During the compilation and rewriting process I discovered there were several scripture passages and stories that received a great deal of my attention over the years – for example, the story of the life of King David, 1 Corinthians 13, the parable of the Prodigal Son, Philippians 2, and James 1 and 2. Those passages have been favorites for much of my life, so I guess there should be no surprise I found them important to meditate on and contemplate. Hopefully each reference will have sufficiently different insights that you will not find these repetitions distracting.

My fondest hope is that somewhere in these pages you will discover some small seed of an idea that will touch your heart and be useful in your personal spiritual journey. Putting this volume together has forced me to invigorate my own personal spiritual growth, because at best I am still very much a work in progress.

Newman's prayer touched me so deeply, that I have chosen to include it both here and on the back cover of this work, so you will be able to quickly and easily find it, time and again. I encourage you to pray it often, reflect thoughtfully on the depth of its meaning in your life, and share it with those you love. *The Mission of My Life* was the clear inspiration for this book.

The Mission of My Life

by Blessed John Henry Cardinal Newman

God has created me to do Him some definite service.
He has committed some work to me which He has not
committed to another.
I have my mission.
I may never know it in this life,
but I shall be told it in the next.
I am a link in a chain,
a bond of connection between persons.
He has not created me for naught.
I shall do good; I shall do His work.
I shall be an angel of peace,
a preacher of truth in my own place,
while not intending it if I do but keep His commandments.
Therefore, I will trust Him,
Whatever I am, I can never be thrown away.
If I am in sickness, my sickness may serve Him;
In perplexity, my perplexity may serve Him.
If I am in sorrow, my sorrow may serve Him.
He does nothing in vain.
He knows what He is about.
He may take away my friends.
He may throw me among strangers.
He may make me feel desolate,
Make my spirits sink,
Hide my future from me.
Still, He knows what He is about.

Reflection

I

The Journey Begins with Baptism

Go therefore and make disciples of all nations,
baptizing them in the name of the Father and of the
Son and of the Holy Spirit. (Matthew 28:19)

For 25 years or so I have spent a great deal of time reading, studying, reflecting on, and writing and speaking about what it means to be a leader in the context of my Catholic Christian faith. Those life obligations are clearly not my idea; rather, they become our responsibilities as part of our gift of Baptism. In the Roman Catholic Rite of Baptism, the celebrant prays these words as he anoints the newly baptized with chrism:

> God the Father of our Lord Jesus Christ has freed
> you from sin, given you a new birth by water and the
> Holy Spirit, and welcomed you into His holy people.
> He now anoints you with the chrism of salvation.
> As Christ was anointed Priest, Prophet, and King,
> so may you live always as a member of His body,
> sharing everlasting life. Amen

As Catholics, we are baptized priests, prophets and kings! Let me say this another way…we *are anointed* priest, prophet and king. What do these words really mean and why is it important that we each internalized the responsibilities of priest, prophet and king?

1

In the opening of his Sermon entitled, "The Three Offices of Christ," Blessed John Henry Cardinal Newman quotes Psalm 45:3-4:

You are the most handsome of men; fair speech has graced your lips, for God has blessed you forever. Gird your sword upon your hip, mighty warrior! In splendor and majesty ride on triumphant!

Then he observes:

Our Lord is here spoken of in two distinct characters. As a teacher, "fair speech has graced your lips" and as conqueror "Gird your sword upon your hip;" or in other words, as a Prophet and as a King. His third special office, which is brought before us…is that of a Priest, in that He offered Himself up to God the Father as a propitiation for our sins. These are the three chief views which are vouchsafed to us of His Mediatorial office; and it is often observed that none before Him has, even in type or resemblance, borne all three characters. Melchizadek, for instance, was a priest and a king, but not a prophet. David was a prophet and king but not a priest. Jeremiah was a priest and prophet, but not a king. Christ was Prophet, Priest, and King. Thus, when our Lord came on earth in our nature, He combined together offices and duties most dissimilar. He suffered, yet He triumphed. He thought and spoke, yet He acted. He was humble and despised, yet He was a teacher. He has at once a life of hardship like the shepherds, yet is wise and royal as the eastern sages who came to do honor to His birth.

St. Matthew tells the story of the mother of James and John asking Jesus for a favor, specifically that He command that her two sons be seated on either side of Him in paradise. Jesus' reply to her suggested she might not really understand what she was asking. He then asked James and John if they could drink the cup He was about to drink. They, of course, responded they could. Jesus assured them they would drink the cup, but continued by saying that He was not the one who would decide where they would sit; rather it would be God, His Father. Jesus then told them:

> *Whoever wishes to be great among you shall be your*
> *servant; whoever wishes to be first among you shall*
> *be your slave. Just so, the Son of Man did not come to*
> *be served but to serve and to give his life as a ransom*
> *for many. (Matthew 20:26-28)*

Whoever wishes to be great must be a servant. The Son of Man, the immortal Priest, Prophet and King, did not come to be served but to serve!

Could the message be any clearer? We are to serve; we are to be servants. Our initiation into 'servant-hood' is our Baptism, when we are anointed priest, the primary definition of which is servant. Fortunately, we are not sent out to live this vocation unarmed, unprepared or without example. Rather, Jesus and the many holy men and women who have preceded us as members of the communion of saints, are wonderful role models for us to emulate as we are challenged to live as servants.

Throughout the Old Testament, some of God's special *servants* are *prophets* – they are the selected few God chose to proclaim His truth to His people. *Truth tellers*, such as Samuel, Elijah, Isaiah, Jeremiah, Daniel and Ezekiel, to name a few, each played significant roles in the history of the Israelites. We, too, are called to be prophets – modern day prophets. Could there ever be a time in our history when "truth telling" is more important than today? In this era of constant "spinning," telling the truth, regardless of

3

where we are, who we are with, what we are doing, or in what circumstances we find ourselves, can be both difficult and often confusing. Constantly repeating (or hearing) the same lie over and over again does not constitute truth even though many people are fooled into accepting it as such. Honest efforts to be real truth tellers are, frankly, looked on with disdain by many who prefer their own version of the truth. Yet, in spite of the challenges, each of us must very deliberately dedicate ourselves to telling God's truth, supporting the truth, and courageously opposing the lies and deceptions that bombard us and our families every day. Set in the context of Nazi Germany, German theologian, Dietrich Bonhoeffer said, "Silence in the face of evil is itself evil. God will not hold us guiltless. Not to speak is to speak. Not to act is to act." We are able to speak the truth when we cling to the sacramental grace of Baptism and allow ourselves to be bolstered by the courage given us through the power of the Holy Spirit in Confirmation.

Telling the truth requires great courage and most of us are fearful. But God knows our weaknesses. Why else would some form of the phrase "do not be afraid" appear in scripture precisely 366 times – one time for each day of the year, including leap day – to encourage us!! While He was on earth, Jesus frequently encouraged His disciples to be courageous. Recently, within a few days of one another I was reminded of two remarkable stories encouraging us to put our full faith and trust in Jesus when we are afraid. The first was in Matthew 14:25-31:

During the fourth watch of the night, he came toward them, walking on the sea. When the disciples saw him walking on the sea they were terrified. "It is a ghost," they said, and they cried out in fear. At once Jesus spoke to them, take courage, it is I; do not be afraid." Peter said to him in reply, "Lord, if it is

4

*you, command me to come to you on the water." He
said, "Come." Peter got out of the boat and began
to walk on the water toward Jesus. But when he saw
how strong the wind was he became frightened; and,
beginning to sink, he cried out, "Lord, save me!"
Immediately Jesus stretched out his hand and caught
him, and said to him, "**O** you of little faith, why did
you doubt?"*

What is it really like to faithfully follow Jesus? Like
Peter, I have often felt Jesus inviting me to step out or take
a leap of faith. In a rush of adrenaline, I am all in and go
for it, and all seems fine for a while. Then, I realize that I
might be in over my head and begin to doubt. Did I hear the
Lord correctly? Maybe I should have "zigged" instead of
"zagged." Whatever the situation, my eyes were opened to
the stormy sea beneath my feet and I frantically call out for
His help. When He comes, the wind dies down, and all is
calm again. I know what it feels like to be fearful because I
am very often unwilling to "Let go and let God."

The second reminder about how much courage it takes to
be faithful happened while carefully studying Rembrandt's
masterpiece entitled "The Storm on the Sea of Galilee." The
painting depicts the story recorded in Mark 4:37-41:

*A violent squall came up and waves were breaking
over the boat, so that it was already filling up. Jesus
was in the stern, asleep on a cushion. They woke him
and said to him, "Teacher, do you not care that we
are perishing?" He woke up, rebuked the wind, and
said to the sea, "Quiet! Be still!" The wind ceased
and there was great calm. Then he asked them, "Why
are you terrified? Do you not yet have faith?" They
were filled with great awe and said to one another,
"Who then is this whom even wind and sea obey?"*

5

My friend Dusty Staub, in his book, *The Seven Acts of Courage*, says quite emphatically that courage is at the very heart of what it means to be a leader, to be a servant. To his argument, I would add that if courage is the heart, then humility is the soul of being a servant. As Catholics, as Christians, we have responsibilities to serve and be truth tellers both of which require ample quantities of courage and humility.

Throughout His ministry on earth, Jesus spoke frequently about what we need to do in order to share in His kingdom. For example, Jesus tells us:

Blessed are they who are persecuted for righteousness, for theirs is the Kingdom of Heaven. (Matthew 5:10)

So if there is a kingdom, there must be a *King*. Jesus clearly was neither talking about an earthly kingdom or king, nor are the words of earthly kingship prayed over us at our Baptism. The kingdom spoken of here is one that is primarily about our stewardship, our spirituality, our living the Gospel, using all the gifts we have been given. In short, for us to live in the kingship of Jesus, we must imitate, to the best of our ability, the whole of the life He modeled for us. Only by imitating Him do we truly live our baptismal responsibility of royal kingship.

In living the challenges of priest, prophet and king we need not be concerned that others might consider us heroes or saints. Nor do we need to worry whether others see us as leaders, regardless of how you might define leader. Luke 13:20-21 recalls that Jesus said:

To what shall I compare the kingdom of God? It is like yeast that a woman took and mixed with three measures of wheat flour until the whole batch of dough was leavened.

6

The yeast was not visible; it did not add significantly to the weight of the mixture. But the yeast did its job – and did it quickly. Even though we have God-given jobs to do, we do not need to be recognized – we just need to do the work, be the leavening, be a sort of spiritual biochemistry. When the job is done, does it really matter who gets credit? Does it really matter whether I get credit? So long as I am an effective catalyst, my job is done and God is glorified.

How do we put ourselves totally before God and prepare or fashion ourselves to be His hands and feet on earth? When Michelangelo was asked how he could possibly turn the enormous block of marble called by many sculptors, *The Giant*, into the magnificent seventeen-foot tall statue of David, he said, "Every block of stone has a statue inside it and it is the task of the sculptor to discover it." God is the sculptor. We are the blocks of marble. If we allow Him to chip away all those pieces of the block that are not authentically us, He will turn us into the masterpieces that we are fully capable of being. With the help of the Holy Spirit, we can be the priests, prophets and kings we were baptized to be. St. Paul tells us in 1 Corinthians 2:9:

What eye has not seen, and ear has not heard, and what has not entered the human heart, what God has prepared for those who love him.

What God has prepared for us for eternity starts now, here, in this life, with these people around us, with these challenges, with these restrictions, with these sufferings, with these joys.

Baptism is our initiation into Christ's Mystical Body. As members of His body we have significant roles and responsibilities that are conferred upon us as part of God's unfathomably complicated grand plan for us that spans all time. He calls us to carry out the plan He designed exclusively for us and no one else. That plan can only be carried out in the context of our baptismal responsibilities to serve, to be truth tellers, and be the finest stewards possible of all the gifts the Father has given us. To reach the Kingdom of Heaven, those responsibilities must be alive in every word we speak and in every action we take.

Reflection

II

Pride, Humility and a Third-Class Ticket on the Stagecoach

❦

The reward of humility and fear of the Lord are riches, honor and life. (Proverbs 22:4)

Philippians 2:1-11 says:

If there is any encouragement in Christ, any solace in love, any participation in the Spirit, any compassion and mercy, complete my joy by being of the same mind, with the same love, united in heart, thinking one thing. Do nothing out of selfishness or out of vainglory; rather humbly regard others as more important than yourselves, each looking out not for his own interest, but (also) everyone for those of others.

*Have among yourselves the same attitude that is also yours in Christ Jesus, Who, though he was in the form of God did not regard equality with God, something to be grasped. Rather, he **emptied** himself, taking the form of a slave, coming in human likeness and found human in appearance, he **humbled** himself, becoming obedient to death, even death on a cross. Because of this, God greatly exalted him and bestowed on him the name that is above every other name, that at the name of Jesus every knee should bend, of those in heaven and on earth and under the* *earth, and every tongue confess that Jesus Christ is Lord, to the glory of God the Father.*

I have read and listened to this passage countless times over the years, but a few years ago I came to a new understanding of it. I would like to share some of those new insights, and what I now believe is required of me (and you as well) if we are to cast off pride and put on the cloak of humility, thus living the way God intended and Jesus modeled for us.

In a work entitled, *The Parables and The Sentences*, written in the twelfth century, Saint Bernard of Clairvaux wrote about the *Follies of Pride*. He said:

> One sort of pride is blind, a second is vain, and a third both blind and vain. Pride is blind when a person thinks there is in him what is not there. It is vain when he glories in the fact that people take him to be what he is not. And it is both blind and vain when he glories inwardly and seeks the respect of others for having a good which he does not possess.

The "vainglory" kind of pride spoken about in Philippians is all about inordinate self-esteem, self-importance, conceit, arrogance, or showing disdain for those considered as inferior to ourselves. More than fifty times in the Old and New Testaments we are cautioned about the dangers and pitfalls of pride. The story of Adam and Eve in the Garden of Eden is the first such story. Wasn't it their desire to "be like God" that led both Adam and Eve to be duped by the serpent to eat the fruit of the tree in the middle of the garden? In a very real sense, the first sin committed by humanity was a sin of pride.

Another very popular story in which the vainglory form of pride played a key role is the story of David (in 1 and 2 Samuel). Much of David's story is very uplifting and encouraging. Who could deny the magnificent beauty of the Psalms, at least half of which were written by David. They are a mixture of truly inspirational songs of thanksgiving and gratitude for what God had done for him, but also songs of sorrow, fear, and virtually all other human emotions. Yet in spite of David's good fortune, we are told David caved to temptation. His own sense of self worth, conceit and arrogance got the best of him. As he gazed upon the beautiful Bathsheba, wife of Uriah, one of his soldiers, he allowed his lustful desires to overtake what he knew was right. David took Bathsheba for his own and had an affair with her; arranged for Uriah to be killed; and then married her. David's undisciplined opinion of himself led him to believe he could have whatever he wanted – such is the very telling evidence of out-of-control pride. Any wonder that pride is one of the seven deadly sins? Often pride is the first one listed. Are not each of us guilty of doing the same thing from time to time?

Do you remember the legend of the little Dutch boy who struggled to plug holes in a leaky dike using his fingers? He did so to save his town from the eminent flooding that would surely occur because the erosive force of larger leaks would eventually weaken the dike and cause it to fail. Having spent almost all of my adult life in the water resources engineering and science arena, I find it useful to use mental images from that background to help myself understand the challenges I face personally.

No matter how much I work to plug holes in the dikes that shore up my personal spirituality, I constantly seem to find others. Just as soon as I think I have one leak stopped, another starts. Even more frustrating is discovering that there are some leaks that have been there for years (maybe even a lifetime) that I have never even noticed before. Those leaks only become apparent when they get so large that it is impossible for me to miss them – translate that statement to mean that I find critical defects in myself that negatively impact my ability to do what God challenges me to do as a Christian, as a Catholic. Possibly the most perplexing new leaks in my spirituality dike are actually old leaks that I thought I had plugged tightly years ago, but they begin to flow again! Some might say such weakness is simply human, and maybe that is so, but the challenges of being a 'real' Christian should never be clouded by such dismissive thinking. We need to honestly face the fact that short-comings in our behavior and deficiencies in our spirituality are traceable to choices we make – one at a time – and those choices have consequences.

One of the most perplexing issues inhibiting my personal spirituality is *pride*. I am not talking about the kind of pride that motivates me to do good work, or the kind of pride that is the internal reward for serving others, or the pride that fills me to the brim when someone I love or care about exceeds all reasonable expectation. I am talking instead about the pride that leads to boasting; the kind that leads to haughty thoughts and feelings about myself; the kind of pride that often leads to inordinate self-esteem; the kind that usually leads me to believe that my needs are far more important than yours. I am not sure whether I simply never recognized that weakness, or whether I saw it all along and chose to ignore it. In reflecting back on my life, my career, etc., I distinctly recall many incidences when that insidious form of pride caused me to do hurtful things; to say things that where hurtful and/or demeaning; and to think thoughts that were unproductive because they gave me an inappropriate sense of worth – so much so that I could easily justify, in my own mind, that I was clearly above others in my position, my ability and my service to mankind!

As I reflect back on some of the most obvious of those situations, rolling my eyes back into my head as I do so, I usually serve up heaping platters of platitudes, working hard to convince myself that I am no longer there and in fact I have moved beyond that phase of my life. Took me quite a while to realize that each time I convinced myself I had moved beyond destructive self-pride, and reveled in my personal growth and development, I actually slipped right back into the same controlling behavior rut.

Proverbs 3:34 warns:

> *The Lord detests all the proud of heart. Be sure of this: They will not go unpunished.*

Thankfully, there is an extremely effective single antidote for pride, and that is *humility* – a word I have used often in my life, but a concept I have not really understood thoroughly or practiced particularly well. From Proverbs 16:12 and 22:4, we are specifically advised that,

> *Before his downfall a man's heart is proud, but humility comes before honor,*

and we are encouraged that,

> *The reward of humility and fear of the Lord are riches, honor and life.*

Think about these two passages. The messages are clear – pride is our downfall, yet when we lead humble lives the Lord will reward us for all eternity. Sounds like a pretty fool proof formula, doesn't it? Be humble, not proud – but why is it so hard? Could it be that we are bombarded from every direction by a me-centered society?

The dictionary provides several definitions for humility including meekness, modesty, unassuming, and not pretentious. I must admit each creates significant challenges for me, in spite of my intellectual awareness of what is required to be spiritually rich. I have always been much too quick to justify and write off my weaknesses as simply *humanum est errare* (to error is human). Down in my core, however, I know that my spiritual strength must be demonstrated through both a genuine humility of spirit and humility in deed.

Let's examine for a minute how that spiritual strength must be played out each day, by way of some questions worth considering regularly:

- Do I seek to serve others rather than expecting to be served?
- Do I use my energy to build others up rather than tear them down?
- Do I treat others with dignity and respect regardless of how they treat me and make their welfare my top priority?
- Am I ethical in all my dealings, regardless of the circumstances?
- Do I selflessly share the gifts I have been given with others?
- Do I look for the good in others?
- Have I allowed myself to be vulnerable?
- Have I shown genuine appreciation to those who have reached out physically and emotionally to me?
- Am I looking out for the benefit of those who are being treated unfairly?
- Am I speaking up when I hear another being spoken of disrespectfully?
- Have I apologized sincerely when my words or deeds offended others?
- Do I elevate the hopes, needs and aspirations of others to the same level as my own?
- What have I done today to serve those around me?
- Do I listen with the intent of really hearing what others say?
- Have I valued the suggestions of others?

- Have I been diligent in sensing the feelings of others?
- Have I looked for opportunities to lend an empathetic ear to another who needs to "vent" or "unload"?
- Have I been aware when my words and/or actions may have caused someone angst or pain?
- What have I done today to promote a sense of hope in those around me?

Referring back to Philippians 2:3-4:

Do nothing out of selfishness or out of vainglory; rather humbly regard others as more important than yourselves, each looking out not for his own interest, but (also) everyone for those of others.

These concepts are foundational for Christians but reach far beyond Christianity and serve as core beliefs of many other faiths as well. Not a real surprise. In his book, *Ethics for the New Millennium*, for example, The Dalai Lama says:

It is also important to realize that transforming the heart and mind so that our actions become spontaneously ethical requires that we put the pursuit of virtue at the heart of our daily lives. This is because love and compassion, patience, generosity, humility, and so on are all complementary.

The Dalai Lama is telling us that though we often find it difficult to remove negative emotions and behavior from our lives, we must do so by making a habit of doing their opposite. For example, if we want to be humble, we must drive out pride in all of its forms.

Stephen Covey, author of *The 7 Habits of Highly Effective People*, maintains:

Humility truly is the mother of all virtues...It unleashes all other learning, all growth and process.

With humility…we're empowered to learn from the past, have hope for the future, and act with confidence in the present.

How does such a thought convert to everyday life? Warren Bennis, says:

Humble people are notable for their self-possession. They know who they are, have healthy egos, and find greater joy in what they do as opposed to the position they hold. They take compliments with a grain of salt and take intelligent criticism without rancor. Such people learn from their mistakes and don't harp on the mistakes of others. They are gracious winners and losers.

Reading or hearing such a comment, some might come away with the notion that being humble is a way to get trampled by society, but humility is neither weakness nor passivity. In fact, humility is a disciplined strength. For quite a few years, in the leadership training and coaching work I do, I have challenged clients to elevate all those around them – the term I use is "show them greatness." Showing greatness is really about treating others with dignity and respect and valuing their humanity because they were created by God, the same as we were created by God.

Several years ago while listening to a homily preached at my home parish, one sentence simply screamed at me. Father stated, "Humility is the soul of greatness." At the very moment I heard those words, I realized that the most fundamental meaning of granting greatness to another, regardless of who or where they are, or what they have done, really only comes to life when we humble ourselves before others. What a challenging thought! What a challenging call to action!

As Catholic Christians we have the responsibility of being role models for everyone around us, serving their legitimate needs, and being respectful of all we encounter. But in living out these responsibilities, there is an interesting paradox that complicates our desire to be truly effective. In his book, *The Leadership Wisdom of Jesus*, Charles Manz says:

> Greatness comes more from avoiding greatness, rather than from seeking it. Or maybe more accurately, the seeds of greatness derive from humility and service. Don't seek honor. Rather, let it seek you in its own way and when the time is right. Don't even think about it. Go about your business pursuing constructive work and focus on honoring and recognizing the contributions of others rather than your own. If you do this sincerely, your efforts will often receive the recognition they deserve, and more, as long as you don't seek and expect it.

Similarly, Nathaniel Hawthorne observed:

> Happiness is as a butterfly which, when pursued, is always beyond our grasp, but which, if you will sit down quietly, may alight upon you.

Precisely the same comment could be made of humility. Go about your business pursuing constructive work focusing on others – and humility will "find" you!

The message for me is simple – when I act with true humility I act without arrogance or excessive pride in myself or in my own achievements. By contrast, when I allow myself to get caught up in my own importance, I quickly slip into vanity – a very real and dangerous form of pride – and vanity both clouds my spiritual growth and impedes my ability to act effectively. The only true antidote to vanity is – you guessed it – humility.

Being humble can be as simple as saying *thank you*. Doing so is clearly good manners and an important social grace, but in reality, it is far more than that. A sincere expression of gratitude for a kindness, for being served, for a gift, for support of any kind is also an act of thoughtfulness and humility. When we say a simple, but genuine, "Thank you," we send the messages "I value you" and "my relationship with you is important." When you thank a perfect stranger you send a loud and clear message about who they are and who you are as a person. How better to lift someone up and let them know how you appreciate them than to acknowledge their presence, their humanity, their inherent value? Sounds like what Jesus modeled for us throughout His life on earth.

Earlier I mentioned that humility is a disciplined strength, and clearly it is. Being humble often requires a great deal of courage because emptying ourselves requires that we be vulnerable – and that is hard to do. But the result of doing so simultaneously increases humility and decreases excessive pride and arrogance, two sins that hold us back and hamper our growth.

Several years ago a priest friend delivered a beautiful homily on the passage from Philippians quoted at the beginning of this reflection. During his sermon, I had one of those lightening bolt revelations that comes to each of us from time to time. Father reread the passage about Jesus in Philippians 2:6, which says, *"He emptied himself and took the form of a slave, being born in the likeness of men."* Then verse eight which says, *"It was thus that he humbled himself, obediently accepting even death, death on a cross!"* Hearing those two verses, spoken back-to-back, I began to understand, for the very first time in my life, just what humility is. In a very real sense, these two verses are exactly parallel; it is almost as though they were written as a mathematical equation. "He emptied himself" equals "He humbled himself." How much clearer could it be? To be humble is to empty one's self. For me to be humble, I must empty myself for others. It is not about me; rather, humility is about my willingness to do what Jesus did. *"Greater love has no one than this, that he lay down his life for his friends" (John 15:13).*

I now know in my heart of hearts that pride is likely the most freely flowing leak in my spiritual dike – and a habit that serves no useful purpose. In fact, if I ever expect to achieve what God has planned for me, I can do so only by being humble. Humility requires me to stop centering on myself and my needs and focus instead on the needs of others. Humility provides the courage I need to apologize sincerely. Humility helps me to encourage others to step forward, even in front of me. Humility gives me the strength to live with an abundance mentality. Humility forces me to see the potential in others – and do what is needed to help them achieve their potential. And humility is the foundation for the courage and honesty that allows me to want to make a real difference rather than wanting to be *personally recognized* for making a difference. I cannot become humble by simply talking about being humble. The only way to grow is through humble thought, word and deed. And to be clear, becoming humble is not a destination, it is an ongoing journey.

While examples of humility are not nearly as visible these days as examples of arrogance, there are some notable exceptions. For instance, in the April 2006 edition of *Guidepost*, Bob Macauley, founder of AmeriCares, a relief organization that distributes critical medicines and medical supplies to the world's poor in times of disaster, tells the story of how he was taught to be a beggar – a lesson in humility if there ever was one – by Mother Theresa, herself. Macauley had done plenty of fundraising at the executive level, but Mother Theresa really showed him how. About thirty five years, ago Macauley and Mother Theresa were on a commercial flight from Guatemala to Mexico to tend to the needs of the poor. (With her strong Albanian accent, Mother Theresa could not pronounce Macauley's first name, Bob – she called him "Bub".) When the flight attendant brought the in-flight meal to Mother Theresa, she asked, "How much does this meal cost?" The flight attendant shrugged. "I don't know, about one dollar in US currency, I suspect." "If I give it back to you," Mother asked, "would you give me that dollar to give to the poor?"

The flight attendant looked startled, "I don't know if I can, it is not something we normally do." Macauley put down his fork as the flight attendant left her cart and went to the front of the plane to consult with the pilot. A few minutes later she returned to us. "Yes, Mother," she said. "You may have the money for the poor." "Here you are." Mother Theresa handed her the tray. Macauley gave the attendant his as well, knowing he couldn't possibly eat in peace with Mother Theresa next to him. One by one, all 129 passengers and crew gave back their meals, so Mother Theresa could have the money for the poor. When they arrived at their destination, she said to Bub, "Get me the food." "What will you do with 129 airline meals?" "Well," said Mother Theresa, "they can't use them any more, so we will take the meals to the poor." So Bob asked the airline, and got the meals – all the while wondering how they would get the food to those in need. Then Mother Theresa said to Macauley – "Get me that airline truck." Long story short, the airlines gave her use of the truck and she and Bob took off for a poor section of town to give the meals and money to the poor, with her behind the wheel driving! Bob's lesson from the incident was that God will give you the power to do anything – including humbling yourself to beg shamelessly – if you are doing it for the right reason.

The work and humble example of Mother Theresa are clearly inspirational, but sometimes we need closer, more personal examples to have our consciences sensitized. My wife and I had such an experience several years ago in the person of one of the most wonderful and truly humble men that she and I have ever met. Father Herald, a member of the Franciscan Friars of the Renewal, was in Atlanta to preach a Lenten Mission at our parish and for the week he was in town he was a guest in our home. We got to see first hand what humility is in action. In addition to being a wonderful homilist, he is kind, magnanimous, truly down-to-earth and connected; fully present to each person he encounters, and dedicated to the physical and spiritual well-being of others, including the poorest of the poor in Honduras, like Mother Theresa was to those in India. We also came to understand, first hand, that four to five hours of prayer each day is standard for him. We commented to each other that humility seemed to ooze from Father Herald's pores – we attributed it to the many hours he spent in prayer.

Several years ago, I was introduced to a prayer, *The Litany of Humility*, written by Raphael Cardinal Merry del Val, Secretary of State for Pope Pius X. While I do not pray it nearly as often as I should, the litany offers an extremely insightful way to increase our spirituality through humility. Each incantation represents some form of earthly challenge that Jesus Himself faced.

O Jesus, meek and humble of heart, hear me.
From the desire of being esteemed, deliver me, Jesus.
From the desire of being loved, deliver me, Jesus.
From the desire of being extolled, deliver me, Jesus.
From the desire of being honored, deliver me, Jesus.
From the desire of being praised, deliver me, Jesus.
From the desire of being preferred to others,
    deliver me, Jesus.

From the desire of being consulted, deliver me, Jesus.

From the desire of being approved, deliver me, Jesus.

From the fear of being humiliated, deliver me, Jesus.

From the fear of being despised, deliver me, Jesus.

From the fear of suffering rebukes, deliver me, Jesus.

From the fear of being calumniated, deliver me, Jesus.

From the fear of being forgotten, deliver me, Jesus.

From the fear of being ridiculed, deliver me, Jesus.

From the fear of being wronged, deliver me, Jesus.

From the fear of being suspected, deliver me, Jesus.

That others may be loved more than I, Jesus, grant me the grace to desire it.

That others may be esteemed more than I, Jesus, grant me the grace to desire it.

That, in the opinion of the world, others may increase and I may decrease, Jesus, grant me the grace to desire it.

That others may be chosen and I set aside, Jesus, grant me the grace to desire it.

That others may be praised and I go unnoticed, Jesus, grant me the grace to desire it.

That others may be preferred to me in everything, Jesus, grant me the grace to desire it.

That others may become holier than I, provided that I may become as holy as I should, Jesus, grant me the grace to desire it.

I find this prayer to be profoundly compelling and sometimes quite scary.

Peter 5:5 and Ephesians 4:1-2:

God is opposed to the proud, but gives grace to the humble.

and

I, then, a prisoner for the Lord, urge you to live in a manner worthy of the call you have received with all humility and gentleness, with patience, bearing with one another through love.

Saint John Paul II, addressing priests and religious of the world (this wisdom, however, applies equally to each of us initiated into the body of Christ and hence anointed priest, prophet and king), said:

... bear witness... not so much in words as by the eloquent language of a transfigured life, capable of amazing the world...

So...what about the stagecoach ticket? And how could that possibly be relevant to this reflection and how could it be connected to the issues of pride and humility?

Back in the days of stagecoaches, one of the first forms of mass transportation in the United States, it seems that tickets could be purchase by class, much like airline tickets are today. Only in the stagecoach era, you could buy a first-class, second-class, or third-class ticket for your journey. Needless to say, provisions and conditions were different with each class. With a first class ticket, you got a seat on the stagecoach, and if the stage broke down, you got to remain in your seat, regardless. If your ticket was second class, you got a seat, but if the coach broke down, you would be asked to exit the coach and stand aside while repairs were made or physical obstacles such as water, mud or downed trees were dealt with. But if you could only afford a third class seat, when difficulties happened, you were required to exit the coach and help the driver and shotgun rider to get it back in motion, even if it meant helping to lift it, push it out of mud, repair broken wheels, axles, etc. – whatever it took. It sounds pretty hard, doesn't it?

As Catholic Christians, we are not given the opportunity to buy first or second class tickets for our journey to eternity. The only class of ticket available is third class. (I regret I have been unable to find the source of this story, so am unable to give proper credit to its author.)

Blessed John Newman speaks of this very same thing at the conclusion of his *Meditation on Christian Doctrine:*

> If I am in sickness, my sickness may serve Him; in perplexity, my perplexity may serve Him; if I am in sorrow, my sorrow may serve Him. My sickness, or perplexity, or sorrow may be necessary causes of some great end, which is quite beyond us. He does nothing in vain. He may prolong my life, He may shorten it; He knows what He is about. He may throw me among strangers, He may make me feel desolate, make my spirits sink, hide the future from me – still He knows what He is about.

Reflection

III

Love God – Love Your Neighbor

You shall love the Lord, your God, with all your heart, with all your soul, and with all your mind. This is the greatest and the first commandment. The second is like it: You shall love your neighbor as yourself.
(Matthew 22:38-39)

Love is arguably the most well-known of the three theological virtues. In reflecting on the topic of love, I have been deeply influenced recently by Peter Kreeft's, *The God Who Loves You*, one of the most beautiful books I have ever read. I first read it while on a silent retreat several years ago.

To set the stage for this reflection on love, let me share one of the best loved passages in the entire New Testament, 1 Corinthians, Chapter 13:

If I speak in human and angelic tongues but do not have love, I am a resounding gong or a clashing cymbal. And if I have the gift of prophecy and comprehend all mysteries and all knowledge; if I have all faith so as to move mountains but do not have love, I am nothing. If I give away everything I own, and if I hand my body over so that I may boast but do not have love, I gain nothing. Love is patient, love is kind. It is not jealous, (love) is not pompous, it is not inflated, it is not rude, it does not seek its own interests, it is not quick-tempered, it does not brood over injury, it does not rejoice over wrongdoing but rejoices with the truth. It bears all things, believes all things, hopes all things, endures all things. Love never fails. If there are prophecies, they will be brought to nothing; if tongues, they will cease; if knowledge, it will be brought to nothing. For we know partially and we prophesy partially, but when the perfect comes, the partial will pass away. When I was a child, I used to talk as a child, think as a child, reason as a child; when I became a man, I put aside childish things. At present we see indistinctly, as in a mirror, but then face to face. At present I know partially; then I shall know fully, as I am fully known. So faith, hope, love remain, these three; but the greatest of these is love.

Throughout the original Greek text of this epistle, the word that we translate as love is *agape*. We might do well to remind ourselves about the meaning of *agape*, but also contrast it with the other three Greek words for love. *Eros* is the romantic form of love, and is the root word for the English word erotic. *Eros* is a form of love that we have little control over; it is one of those phenomena that sweeps over us. An extreme case of *eros* is love-at-first-sight. If that ever happened to you, you will recall how little control you had over your emotions. *Eros* is a form of love that is deeply rooted in emotion. The second word for love in the wonderfully complex Greek language is *philos* – the root for a brotherly form of love, for example Philadelphia, the city of brotherly love. For whatever reason, we seem to have at least some control over the *philos* (or friendship) form of love, but it is not an emotional kind of love in the same vein as *eros*. *Philos* in some respects is a *quid quo pro* type of love – very real, but not really emotional. *Storge* is a form of love that we have little control over and it, too, is a form of love or affection that tends to sweep over us. An example of *storge* is the warm emotional feelings we have when we see a new baby, a beautiful child, or experience the love of a relative or friend.

The form of love that Jesus modeled for us cannot be adequately defined with any of these three forms of love. It is more than emotion, more than friendship, more than a warm feeling we might get from a pleasant experience. The love Jesus shows is far more complex. The authors of scripture chose to use an ancient Greek word that had nearly fallen out of use to describe it. *Agape* was adopted as the word they would use to describe the essence of God Himself, God's love for us and the form of love that God intends for us to extend to each other. An important distinction about *agape* is that it is NOT an emotion. *Agape* is action and is a conscious choice that each of us makes many times every day to treat others with unconditional dignity and respect no matter what they say or do to us.

Even though there are four distinct words that identify four different forms of love, those forms of love are not necessarily independent of one another. In fact, we can and often do, experience multiple forms of love for each other at the same time. A clear example is evident in the relationship between husband and wife. For a marriage to last, both *eros* and *agape* must be present. While *eros* is clearly the spice of a relationship, and may have been what jump-started the romance, if the relationship is not ultimately founded on *agape* there is trouble ahead. How often do we hear one or both partners in a marriage say they want to go their separate ways because there seems to be no spark in their love life? *Eros* without *agape* is very much like an alcohol fire – poof, a short burst of heat, then little else. *Eros* with *agape*, by contrast lasts, and even when *eros* subsides, the power of *agape* rekindles and very much sustains. From personal experience, I must say that a healthy dose of *philos* between spouses is also a great source of joy. But the willingness to share love unconditionally actually fuels the wonderful power and experience of *eros* and *philos*. God truly knew what He was doing when He created us the way we are!!

As Christians, we believe to our core that God is love. So what does that mean? Very simply, it means that God is *agape* and *agape* is not a feeling, so God is not a feeling. Feelings are actually the dribbles of love that we receive quite passively. Nothing about God is passive. In fact, God is warm, close to us, unconditional, fiery and dynamic. His love for us never fails, it never wavers, it never stops. Our love for Him, by contrast, can be lukewarm, passing, and conditional – but can also be deep, passionate, and dedicated. We need only study the lives of the "capital S" Saints (both ancient and modern-day saints) to know that what separates them from the rest of us, working hard to be "lower case" saints, is their deep and abiding love of God, in all three persons of the Blessed Trinity.

God's love for us is limitless. In fact, His love for each person is so grand that He created each of us with a free will. I would like to make a clear distinction here – God loves each of us, personally, and that is radically more powerful a statement than saying God loves all of humanity. Because He loves each of us, He expects us to love each other, with the same distinction or qualification. While we might find it easy to say that we love our fellow man, or that we love everyone, it is far more difficult to say emphatically that we love our next door neighbor, the person who has been a pain in our neck for years. Loving specifically is far more difficult than loving generally. God's love for us, each one of us, is specific. Jesus modeled that behavior – He loved His persecutors as much as He loves us!!

There are some proofs of God's love that are difficult to understand. For example, God created us with a free will, yet He knows all things even before they happen in our frame of reference (or concept of time). So how could that prove He loves us? First of all, God could, just as easy as not, have created each of us with preprogrammed "mother boards", such as the ones in our personal computers, that would only know how to love Him, and everyone else, i.e., all of our choices would be predetermined. Think about that. Would that be a loving thing for God to do? Wouldn't preprogramming us to love Him actually argue precisely the opposite – that He really does not love us? For those of us who are parents, would demanding love from our children and making all of their decisions for them be an indicator of our love for them? I think not. Instead, such action on our part would show just how insecure we are, how controlling we are, and how little we value our children as individuals. God is not insecure. He values each of us individually. He does not need us to love Him. And, in spite of what many people think, God is not a control freak.

No. God loves us so much that He will NOT impose His will on us. He gives us the choice to love Him – or not. Only a truly loving God would do that. If we were not free to consciously choose whether or not to love our creator, it would not actually be love. It would be something very different. Instead, God gives us the choice, He lets us decide. And, no matter what our decision is, He loves us more than we can imagine.

Even when we choose to separate ourselves from a relationship with Him by serious sin, He still loves us. Amazing, in our sinfulness, He loves us. Because of our sinfulness He sacrificed Himself. He died for our sinfulness. What an incredible dichotomy. We turn our back on God, we snub His boundless love, and in response He endures persecution beyond our imagining. Wow, what a love story.

I have recently found it very useful to reread 1 Corinthians 13 substituting *agape* everyplace *love* appears. Reading the chapter in this way will certainly not flow like the version with which we are familiar. In fact, the reading sounds somewhat foreign and awkward. But maybe there is good reason to go through this exercise because it might just force us to rethink what each of the verses really means in light of God's unconditional love for us. For example:

Agape is patient, agape is kind. It is not jealous, (agape) is not pompous, it is not inflated, it is not rude, it does not seek its own interests, it is not quick-tempered, it does not brood over injury, it does not rejoice over wrongdoing but rejoices with the truth. It bears all things, believes all things, hopes all things, endures all things.

For some reason I have found that reading this passage in this way helps me to begin to more fully understand what *agape* is. Everything about *agape* is selfless and unconditional. The word love that we so casually use in our normal conversation tends to be far too vague, possibly even trite when compared to the real love of God, and too often is about emotion or feelings.

According to Peter Kreeft, in *The God Who Loves You*:

St. Paul has first told us *agape*'s surpassing value so that we would approach this description of its nature with thirst rather than just curiosity. He told us that *agape* is the one thing that gives value to all things. Even the greatest things in the world – supernatural gifts, prophecy, understanding, faith, and the works of love themselves – are nothing without *agape* beating at their heart. *Agape* is *summum bonum*, the greatest good, "the chief end of man", the meaning of life, the alternative to emptiness and "vanity of vanities", the answer to Ecclesiastes and the modern world.

I am reminded of the lyrics of a song made popular by John Denver many years ago "If love never lasts forever, what's forever for?" What is eternity for? Very simply, eternity is for *agape* and absolutely nothing else.

Agape is also the catalyst for all other virtues. For example, without love, it is impossible to be humble. Let me repeat, without love, humility is not possible. Why? Because, above all else (according to Scott Hahn), humility is "loving service to others."

Again from 1 Corinthians 13:

At present we see indistinctly, as in a mirror, but then face to face. At present I know partially; then I shall know fully, as I am fully known. So faith, hope, love remain, these three; but the greatest of these is love.

Even though I have read these verses several hundred times, both silently and aloud, I am not sure I ever really understood the full meaning of these three sentences until recently. About them, Peter Kreeft says that we will likely never fully understand the power and extent to God's love until we are with Him in heaven – that all we understand now will shrink to insignificance when the full truth of God's love in eternity embraces us. Kreeft further asserts that the reason *agape* is the greatest of the three theological virtues (faith, hope and *agape*), is that in heaven, in God's presence, both faith and hope are no longer needed. Faith is the virtue that allows us to believe what we cannot see or prove. In heaven, we will be experiencing the magnificence of the beatific vision. Another way of saying the same thing is that there will be no more need for faith; it will be replaced by the reality of seeing God and being in full presence with Him. There will also no longer be a need for hope, because all that we *hoped* for, fueled by the gift of faith, will be completely fulfilled. Our existence for all eternity then is to live in love – God's love.

31

And, interestingly enough, if we try "eternalizing" anything else (with the exception of *agape*) we spoil it! Eternalize wealth and it goes south. Eternalize *eros*, it eventually becomes a drug that requires ever-increasing doses to avoid boredom. I think you get the point. Only *agape* lasts.

In Matthew 22:36-39, the Pharisees asked Jesus:

Teacher, which commandment in the law is the greatest? He said to him, "You shall love the Lord, your God, with all your heart, with all your soul, and with all your mind. This is the greatest and the first commandment. The second is like it: You shall love your neighbor as yourself."

Love God: love your neighbor. With Jesus' declaration that these two commandments are the greatest, then surely they solidify that God is love, and that God's love is the basis for all loving.

God is Love, and Love itself cannot receive love as a *passivity*, but it can spread as an activity. Remember *agape* is not a feeling – *agape* is action. God, therefore, is Love-in-eternal-activity.

A final thought. One of the most remarkable epiphanies I have experienced in decades happened as I read Kreeft's assertion that **God cannot fall in love**, not because He is less loving than we are but because He is more loving. "He cannot fall in love for the same reason that water cannot get wet: it *is* wet. God *is* love."

32

Reflection

IV

Some Thoughts on Lent, Almsgiving and Freedom

For just as a body without a spirit is dead, so also faith without works is dead. (James 2:26)

I recently heard a story about Abraham Lincoln I had never heard before. Even though Lincoln hated slavery, he did not feel he fully understood the complications of the atrocity. So, without drawing attention to himself during a trip to New Orleans, he managed to slip away and go to a public slave auction. He was horrified at the spectacle – the very core of his being was shaken by what he witnessed. One slave after another was brought in chains to the auctioneer who did his best to drive up the price. A very attractive young slave girl, about twenty years old, was roughly dragged to the center of the stage, her beauty hidden by the anguish, anger and fear on her face. She had been owned by someone else and had been severely abused and now, the entire process was about to begin for her again. Her anger became even more outwardly hostile as the bidding began. First one bidder bid, and then another, higher. Lincoln decided that he would bid as well, and as the bidding continued, he upped his offer each time someone else did. Finally, the gavel fell, and Lincoln was declared the winning bidder. He walked over to the young woman and quietly and humbly stood before her. Clearly her only experience with white men had been violent mistreatment. She sneered at him as he approached.

Lincoln, in a kind and gentle voice, said to her, "Young lady you are free." With malice in her voice she asked him what he meant. He repeated his comment, "You are free." As her anger diminished somewhat, she asked, "Does that mean I can say whatever I want to say?" He gently replied, "Yes, young lady, you can say whatever you want to say." "Does that mean I can do whatever I want to do?" Again Lincoln replied, "Yes, you can do whatever you want to do." "Does that mean I can go wherever I want to go?" "Yes, you can go wherever you want to go." After a period of complete silence, the young woman, with tears running down her cheeks, looked into Lincoln's eyes, and said "Then I choose to go with you."

"You are free." Three simple words, ten letters total, and the slave girl's world was turned upside down. How fortunate she was to have been on the block when honest Abe decided to learn firsthand about the horrors of slave captivity and control – and then chose to get involved. All the violence that had defined the young woman's earlier life, a life over which she had no control, was turned into one filled with hope and promise. She now could choose what she wanted to do with her life. She was truly blessed.

In James 2:14-17, we are told:

> *My Brothers, what good is it to profess faith without practicing it? Such faith has no power to save one, has it? If a brother or sister has nothing to wear and no food for the day, and you say to them," Good-by and good luck! Keep warm and well fed," but do not meet their bodily needs, what good is that? So it is with the faith that does nothing in practice. It is thoroughly lifeless.*

Abraham Lincoln chose to practice his faith the day he bought, then freed the slave girl. What a dramatic action, yet he did not call attention to himself, quite rather the opposite. *The Catechism of the Catholic Church*, in paragraph 1969 says:

> The New Law *practices the acts of religion*: almsgiving, prayer and fasting, directing them to the 'Father who sees in secret,' in contrast with the desire to 'be seen by men.'

The Catechism also teaches (in paragraph 1434) that:

> The interior penance of the Christian can be expressed in many and various ways. Scripture and the Fathers (of the Church) insist above all on three forms, *fasting, prayer,* and *almsgiving*, which express conversion in relation to oneself, to God, and to others. Alongside the radical purification brought about by Baptism or martyrdom they cite as means of obtaining forgiveness of sins: efforts at reconciliation with one's neighbor, tears of repentance, concern for the salvation of one's neighbor, the intercession of the saints, and the practice of charity 'which covers a multitude of sins.'

During the season of Lent, in particular, Holy Mother the Church strongly encourages us to pray, fast and give alms. The first two acts are somewhat self-evident, but the giving of alms, maybe not quite so much. Simply stated, *almsgiving* is the practice of giving money or goods to the poor. It is one of many ways that people practice charity particularly during Lent, but at other times as well. The underlying call for giving of alms in the New Testament is found in 1 Corinthians 13:13,

> *And now faith, hope, and love abide, these three; and the greatest of these is love.*

God has given us all we have – life, love, our abilities and resources. We need to constantly count our blessings, and follow the example of the poor widow from the story in St. Luke's Gospel. You may remember she was the one who put the few small coins she had into the temple treasury. Jesus singled her out as the example for His followers – she gave all she had. Our giving, too, must be generous.

Almsgiving is far more than just giving of our financial resources. Almsgiving must include a full testament of our Catholic Christian stewardship. Stewardship, the personal expression of our spirituality, requires generous use and giving of our time, talent and treasure.

There are many ways to give of our time. Some examples include visiting the sick or imprisoned; spending quality time, particularly spiritual time with your children, or grandchildren, or godchildren. Even participating in parish instructional programs and social events can be included. As Christians, we are known through community so giving our time to activities that enrich community is important. During Lent, extra time in prayer, particularly on behalf of others, is a wonderful way to give of ourselves.

When called to give, do we put our talents to work to serve others, not for pay, but as a gift? Do we donate our talents in service to our parish, neighborhood or community? Using the best of the talents God has given us to help others is an important way to "glorify God through our deeds."

Using our financial treasure for good is probably the most visible and frequently talked about form of almsgiving. Throughout the New Testament, we read about those who are crippled, blind, and otherwise unable to care for themselves, sitting and begging, often outside the doors of the synagogue waiting for the generosity of others. Those same needs exist today and there are numerous charitable organizations that seek our financial help to mitigate those needs. One such organization, active in many Catholic parishes is the St.

Vincent de Paul Society. I'm not sure any of us have a clear understanding of the scope of the assistance and hope the generous donations from even a relatively small parish can have on the less fortunate in the surrounding community. If you do not currently donate to St. Vincent de Paul, consider doing so. If you would rather not donate money to assist with rent or utilities, consider once a month donating a $25 food gift card from one of the local groceries. Or maybe do both! Even when the local group at our parish is short on funds to help with critical necessities, St. Vincent is always willing to provide food cards – fully consistent with Catholic social teaching. If a man is hungry, give him a fish, then teach him to fish so he can provide for himself and his family.

There are many wonderful stories of almsgiving and freedom recorded for us in Holy Scripture. One is the story of the Samaritan woman at the well that Jesus engaged in conversation while asking her for a drink. He then offered her the living water so that she would never thirst. His gift changed her life profoundly. Another is the story about Jesus giving sight to a man who had been blind from birth. Giving him sight was remarkable, but Jesus did not just restore his physical sight, He also gave him the ability to see Jesus as the Christ, the savior of all mankind. Many came to believe as they witnessed the events of that day.

During the season of Lent, we need to reexamine our beliefs, search for understanding, and commit even more deeply to living our faith than during any other time of year, because during Lent, we prepare to celebrate the most amazing gift given mankind in the history of the universe. Jesus came into the world, humbled himself, suffered enormously, and gave His life for us. He suffered and gave His life for me.

While praying the Liturgy of the Hours-Morning Prayers, during the second week of Lent, I was deeply touched by a number of prayers and scripture passages that enriched my understanding and beliefs about God, the truth of Jesus' death and resurrection and the love that Father, Son and Holy Spirit have for me. I would like to share a few of those that touched my heart in hopes you will find them inspirational as well.

The first is a reading from the book of Deuteronomy 7: 6-9:

> *For you are a people holy to the LORD, your God; the LORD, your God, has chosen you from all the peoples on the face of the earth to be a people specially his own. It was not because you are more numerous than all the peoples that the LORD set his heart on you and chose you; for you are really the smallest of all peoples. It was because the LORD loved you and because of his fidelity to the oath he had sworn to your ancestors, that the LORD brought you out with a strong hand and redeemed you from the house of slavery, from the hand of Pharaoh, king of Egypt. Know, then, that the LORD, your God, is God: the faithful God who keeps covenant mercy to the thousandth generation toward those who love him and keep his commandments.*

God's commitment to His chosen people is evident from ancient times to the present and beyond.

The second is from Isaiah 53:11-12:

> *Through his suffering, my servant shall justify many, and their guilt he shall bear. Therefore I will give him his portion among the great, and he shall divide the spoils with the mighty, because he surrendered himself to death and was counted among the wicked: And he shall take away the sins of many, and win pardon for their offenses.*

Three of the Psalm-prayers included during this particular week were simply beautiful:

Lord Jesus, you have revealed your justice to all nations. We stood condemned, and you came to be judged in our place. Send your saving power on us and, when you come in glory, bring your mercy to those for whom you were condemned.

God of mercy and goodness, when Christ called out to you in torment; you heard Him and gave Him victory over death because of His love for you. We already know the affection you have for us; fill us with a greater love of your name, and we will proclaim you more boldly before men and happily lead them to celebrate your glory.

And

Lord, you have renewed the face of the earth. Your Church throughout the world sings you a new song, announcing your wonders to all. Through a virgin, you have brought forth a new birth in our world, through your miracles, a new power; through your suffering, a new patience; in your resurrection, a new hope, and your ascension, new majesty.

A passage from 2 Tim 2:8, 11-13 instructs:

Remember that Jesus Christ, a descendant of David, was raised from the dead. You can depend on this: If we have died with him, we shall also live with him; If we hold out to the end we shall also reign with him. But if we deny him he will deny us. If we are unfaithful he will still remain faithful, for he cannot deny himself.

I was particularly touched by one of the intentions prayed during Morning Prayers these same few days:

> Look with favor on us as we begin our daily work –
> let us be fellow workers with you. Make our work
> today benefit our brothers and sisters – that with them
> and for them we may build an earthly city, pleasing
> to you.

This reflection began with a story about Abraham Lincoln buying a slave girl at auction, then giving the young woman her freedom. Although written about elsewhere ("God's Amazing Love" by Steve Brown, 2000), I must tell you that the authenticity of the story cannot be proven. Yet even if the story did not actually happen, it is a wonderful parallel story that might help us better understand, to some extent, the full significance of the more profoundly powerful story of our being brought out of slavery and given freedom. On a universal scale, the reality of the Father choosing us, tolerating our sinful nature, promising to send His Son to save us, then actually doing so, with the Son suffering inhuman torture and death on a cross so that we could be freed from the bonds of slavery to sin, is true – there is no greater truth. We have been saved by the loving acts of our awesome God.

A final thought comes from Revelation 21:1-5:

> *Then I saw a new heaven and a new earth. The*
> *former heaven and the former earth had passed*
> *away, and the sea was no more. I also saw the holy*
> *city, a New Jerusalem, coming down out of heaven*
> *from God, prepared as a bride adorned for her*
> *husband. I heard a loud voice from the throne saying,*
> *"Behold, God's dwelling is with the human race. He*
> *will dwell with them and they will be his people and*

God himself will always be with them [as their God].
He will wipe every tear from their eyes, and there
shall be no more death or mourning, wailing or pain,
[for] the old order has passed away.

The one who sat on the throne said, *"Behold, I make all things new."* As the chosen people of God, we, too, have been freed from the bonds of slavery, not just for a lifetime but for all eternity.

Will tears flow from my eyes, like those of the slave girl, as I fully embrace my freedom and salvation, generously bestowed on me through the unselfish sacrifices of Jesus?

Reflection

V

Getting to the Heart of Mission and Service

Like good stewards of the manifold grace of God,
serve one another with whatever gift each of you has
received. (1Peter 4:10)

In his book, *Leadership from the Inside Out*, Kevin Cashman relates the story of a priest, who was confronted by a soldier while he was walking down a road in pre-revolutionary Russia. The soldier, aiming his rifle at the priest, commanded "Who are you? Where are you going? Why are you going there?" Unfazed the priest calmly replied, "How much do they pay you?" Somewhat surprised, the soldier responded, "Twenty-five kopecks a month." The priest paused, and in a deeply thoughtful manner said, "I have a proposal for you. I'll pay you fifty kopecks each month if you will stop me here every day and challenge me to respond to *those same three questions.*"

As I got to the end of this story, I smiled as I thought about the simplicity of the message, although in my heart, I was perplexed by the significant complexity of these three questions. In composite, the questions – *Who are you? Where are you going?* and *Why are you going there?* – should force us to focus on some of the most fundamental issues that we deal with as Christians! These three simple questions, taken seriously, should significantly challenge us to probe our innermost personal thoughts and feelings, and bring us face-to-face with our spirituality and the health of our eternal souls.

Often when asked who we are, we tend to focus on the job we do, the position title printed on our business card, or on the honor we may have just received. But is that *really* who we are? I think not. When thinking about who we are, we would be far better served by thinking about the condition of our souls, the essence of our character, the motivations that drive our actions, and the roots of our feelings. Granted the jobs we do are important, but they are only jobs and they come and go. The title on our business card is equally ephemeral. And the honor just conferred, while clearly something to celebrate, fades with time.

Who are we, *really*? We are each children of God, put here on earth, in this very time and place for a specific purpose – to love God and fulfill our part of His grand plan for eternity. As such, Jesus confirmed these truths about each of us – we are special; we each have unique gifts needed by our community that no one else can give; and whenever we choose not to use our gifts in a given situation, the opportunity will be lost for all time. There really are no "Do-overs." In much the same way each snow flake is different and fragile, just like each of us; many joined together (if only by gravity) can stop traffic. So we must be committed to fulfilling our part of God's grand plan. The opening lines of Blessed John Henry Cardinal Newman's beautiful prayer, *The Mission of My Life*, speak directly to our purpose:

> God has created me to do Him some definite service;
> He has committed some work to me which He has
> not committed to another. I have my mission…
> somehow I am necessary for His purposes.

On a very personal note, I believe God has created me to serve in the roles of husband, father, grandfather, brother, uncle and friend – to name a few. My effectiveness in fulfilling these roles is deeply and directly related to my relationship with Him, how I use the gifts and talents He has given me, and the spiritual condition of my soul. It is the same for each of us. However, we would be fools if we did not acknowledge the constant barrage of forces in our lives that eat away at our character and motivations to do good.

To overcome the evils and challenges we face, we simply must stay in touch with God, and concentrate on our relationship with Him. We do that through prayer, meditation, self-reflection and good works, to name just a few of the ways. A word about self-reflection or examination – *it is really, really difficult for most of us*. Nevertheless, it is a key factor in our spiritual growth and it is a dynamic, on-going process. We must each repeat the process over and over as we learn, stumble, fall, get up, learn and grow from our mistakes and move on. Getting to know ourselves well may be one of the most difficult challenges we face in life.

When asked "Where we are going", the usual response is to name our current destination or our short-term goal. A more thoughtful answer might describe the more fundamental question about where our life is headed or where we want it to go, or what we hope our lives will mean. Not surprising though, the first question (Who are you?) is much easier to answer than the second (Where are you going?). This more difficult question asks us to describe a vision for our life, a focus that is so profound that it shapes our thoughts, feelings, motivations, and behavior. The question about where we are going could simply be answered "to heaven." But many of us struggle to set an effective course for such a journey, even when we know at a visceral level that a clear vision would help us get there, especially when we must make tough choices in the midst of conflict, stress and turmoil. Solomon, with his God-given wisdom, understood, advised and wrote in Proverbs 29:1:

The person without vision will soon perish.

Our goal of achieving eternal life with God will be made easier if we give serious thought to what we must do in order to get to heaven, as opposed to simply hoping it will happen. A personal vision of how we plan to build and leave a legacy is a powerful way of guiding us through difficult decisions for reaching our destination. You see, the legacy you leave is the life you lead. Will it be one that leads others to Him – or not? Funny how we have little problem carefully planning where to go on vacation, and ignore (or procrastinate) making far more important decisions about where our lives are going and how to achieve eternal life with God. While attending the funeral of a dear friend recently, I was deeply moved by the opening of the celebrant's homily "Chris walked every step of life with Jesus." What a wonderful legacy to all who knew him.

Somehow, I feel the third and final question the priest offered to pay the soldier to ask him each day – "Why are you going there?" – boils down to a challenge about fully keeping our eyes on the goal, about fully understanding our motivations and meaning which are logical extensions beyond the fundamentals of who we are and what contributions we want to make in life. Are our motivations guided by a genuine desire to love (*agape*) and to serve the legitimate needs of others and to make selfless contributions to our families, parish family, organizations, communities and humankind in general? Or, is our motivation about self-gratification? Is it all about lifting ourselves up at the expense of others? Is it about trying to make ourselves look good in the eyes of others? Or is it really about getting our needs met?

This question about motivation requires that our intentions be coupled with our choice to act. Mahatma Ghandi commented that "The difference between what we do and what we are capable of doing would suffice to solve

46

most of the world's problems." I would add that in taking action on what we are capable of doing we should concentrate our energy on being significant first as an individual, then one-on-one with others. For example, the only way we can improve our effectiveness as Catholic Christian fathers and mothers is to first concentrate on being good Christian men and women. When we concentrate our energies there, we will soon begin to see we are making a difference in the lives of others on a much larger scale.

In August, 1988, I was invited to be a guest speaker at an international water resources conference being held at a beautiful resort on the north coast of Sicily, about 20 miles west of Palermo. While there, my hosts from the Geological Survey of Italy had asked several members of their organization to be my guides, companions, and interpreters. How gracious they were. During a free afternoon, they took me to the city where they worked. One of the highlights of the day for me was a visit to the Duomo Sant'Agata. The cathedral in downtown Catania was built over the very spot where the holy martyr Agatha died in 251 A.D. The current structure dates from 711 A.D. Each time it was damaged during wartime, the church was repair. The Duomo is still in active use and remains incredibly beautiful. As we entered the building through the massive main doors, I got my first glimpse of a painting that covered the enormous arched walls and ceiling behind the altar. My immediate thought was, 'How could anyone paint such a massive and beautiful picture?' After standing in awe for a few minutes, I was drawn-in to examine the painting much more closely. As I walked toward the painting, I discovered that it was not a painting at all, rather a mosaic made of millions of tiles about 1 centimeter square – carefully mounted, one at a time. The artistry was beyond anything I had ever seen. As I got closer, however, I began to see a variety of imperfections. There were chips in some tiles, cracks in the mortar and a variety of discolorations that had not been apparent at a distance. How odd that a work of such beauty had so many imperfections and while still beautiful in composite, was not quite so beautiful close up.

Recently thinking about my trip to Sicily, I could not help but reflect on some interesting and hopefully useful parallels between that experience in Catania and the many issues related to being a Catholic and in responding to that first question "Who are you?" As a child of God, I have been created in His image and likeness – a grand sight to behold. But in my weakness, I choose to do my own will instead of that of the Father, and thus add numerous imperfections to the beautiful masterpiece He created me to be. But in what seems to me to be an amazing paradox, God simultaneously and unconditionally loves and sees me both as His masterpiece and as His child with many faults.

In much the same way that there can be imperfections in the midst of beauty, a dynamic tension exists between and among responsibilities we have as Christians, particularly in the way we interact with and serve each other. For example, we are given the commandment to love everyone and to treat each other with dignity and respect and give them the benefit of the doubt, yet are asked to hold them accountable for their actions.

Similarly, we should be courageous enough to both counsel and be counseled, but avoid being judgmental. We should constantly search our inner selves and be honest enough to reflect on both our strengths and our weaknesses, to use our strengths for good and work to overcome our faults. We should put away false pride and embrace true humility, the kind Jesus modeled for us. We should be dedicated to developing ourselves and others. And we should do each of these with kindness, honesty, courage, and yes, love. We should, as Mother Theresa advised, not worry about doing "big" things, but doing "lots of little things" with great love.

How we choose to live our lives impacts not only us, but those around us. We can positively influence others, leading them to Christ; or we can influence them to be less than they were created to be. Lest we forget, as Catholics, as Christians, we are all called to be role models for those around us. So, as others experience us will they be influenced by our Christian spirit and heritage or will they see in us someone who does not walk their talk? Will there be enough Christ in us that they will not be blinded by our flaws? Will they be willing to help us with our imperfections because they see a greater value in us?

I sincerely hope others will treat me fairly and lovingly and that those around me will give me a chance to serve them and be willing to challenge me along the way. But truthfully, just as the mosaic over the altar in Duomo Sant'Agata requires constant repair and maintenance, I, too, am a work in progress because earthly and societal elements constantly take their toll on me. I need help. External forces of all sorts challenge our spiritual well-being just like war, humidity, seismicity, and negligence have damaged the mosaic in that church in Catania.

The forces working against us take many forms. For example, we often yield to temptations, we might slip into a spiritual malaise, wander away from a compelling vision that gives us direction for achieving eternal life, loose a grip on being guided by principles, fall into a comfortable routine. The list of gravitational forces that move us away from being the kind of person God created us to be goes on and on. Being a Christian requires us to understand that we have taken on never-ending, challenging work. Chris Lowney, in his book, *Heroic Leadership*, observes:

> It (being a Christian) involves the willingness to continue questioning and probing one's approach, tactics, values, and culture.... Being a Christian

often is a swim against the current. And as hard as it is to swim upstream, it becomes all the more difficult once the seductive opportunity to turn around and drift with the flow presents itself.

Yes, our edges may be chipped, our armor chinked, and our surfaces tarnished. But rather than being too disillusioned, we should step back, look at the big picture, be inspired by the inherent beauty God created and sees in us. We must then resolve, with the help of the Holy Spirit, to work on the imperfections and weaknesses that keep us from being our best selves, those that keep us from reaching our full potential and divert us away from our goal of living with our Creator for eternity. Blessed John Newman says in his *Meditations on Christian Doctrine*:

> I am born to serve Thee, to be Thine, to be Thy instrument. Let me be Thy blind instrument. I ask not to see – I ask not to know – I ask simply to be used.

The task of becoming a Christian is never really complete – it is an ongoing process that requires our full attention each day, our openness to the urgings of the Holy Spirit, and a faith that is strong and vibrant.

Let me make the responses to the three simple questions posed by the soldier to the priest more personal. The answers for me come down to this: I am a child of God, created for a specific purpose and so I must lead an exemplary Christian life. My beliefs demand action and my faith challenges me to the limits of my capability and beyond. I must use the gifts given to me and be dedicated to enhancing and refining those gifts. When I fall, which I do frequently, I must get up and move forward with determination. I must commit to interacting with others in ways that leads them to Christ. I cannot sit still. I cannot merely be an observer. I must be completely involved. In much the same way Jesus left an eternal legacy by becoming a man like us, dying, then rising from the dead, we too are challenged to leave a legacy. Could there be a greater legacy than leading a Christian life, leading others to Jesus?

So...Who are you?
Where are you going?
Why are you going there?

I look forward to experiencing the beauty of the mosaic you are creating!

Reflection

VI

Time for Change? No Time Like the Present!

*With people it is impossible, but not with God for all
things are possible with God. (Mark 10:27)*

Do you make New Years resolutions? How about Lenten
resolutions? If so, great, but if not, it is never too late.
Making resolutions and keeping them, however, are two
very different things.

I see resolutions in two flavors. The first is a promise
we make to ourselves or others that we will continue to do
something we already do. For example, my wife and I will
continue to pray together daily. Or as an individual, I will
continue to exercise regularly. Such resolutions are noble,
but they do not usually cause us to stretch ourselves into
positive new behaviors, rather they reinforce existing habits.
Based on our circumstances, such resolutions may be all we
can handle. But most of the time we are capable of more, far
more – if only we would make the effort.

The second type of resolution requires us to develop
new disciplines, new habits, new opportunities to grow. The
operative word here is NEW. We promise ourselves or others
we will start doing something positive, something that will
create value for ourselves, our marriage, our family, etc.
The major stumbling block for such resolutions is that new
actually means *change* – change the way we think, change
the way we feel, change the way we behave, change the way

we respond to others or to situations, change the way we do things, prioritize things, and so on. Typical resolutions of this type include the likes of: I will commit to Eucharistic Adoration one hour per week; I will begin exercising four times per week. I will help my spouse far more than I currently do by (fill in the blank); I will attend Friday Morning Men's Fellowship every week.

Resolutions require change, but many of us prefer to let things rock along as they are because it is easier that way. Interestingly, however, most of us are not 100% satisfied with our lives, all of our relationships; maybe some are not even 100% satisfied with the quality of their marriage. Although we do not have any control over others, we do have control of our own behavior and by changing one side of the dynamic, we could influence the other to reciprocate. An old adage that I often use in my leadership coaching is that, "If you keep on doing what you've always been doing, you'll keep getting what you've always been getting." Explicit in this comment is that if you want a different outcome, you must be willing to *change*! Albert Einstein defined insanity as "doing the same thing over and over again and expecting different results."

Let me walk you through a brief scenario. When you and your spouse were dating and beginning to talk about getting married did you notice your partner had some annoying habits. If so did you ever, even if only for a brief moment, entertain the thought that you could change them? Do you suppose your spouse ever had similar thoughts about you? Did you actually try to change your partner? Or, did you ever try to change the behavior of a colleague at work? Come on!! Did you really? Truth be told, most of us have fallen into that trap, and maybe some of us still think it is possible to change another person. When my wife, Laurel, and I were dating, back in the late '60's, I was a smoker. Laurel did not like cigarettes, did not like being around them, some brands even caused sneezing attacks, coughing, etc. Her dad had smoked, and I smoked. For the nearly three years we dated and about the first 7 years we were married, she tried, in vain, to get me to quit. But instead of quitting I began smoking progressively more, using work as an excuse. Then one day, Amy, our then 2-year old daughter, began greeting me as I came home from work, reaching into her pocket (as she had seen me do many times) pretending to offer me a cigarette, even before saying hello. By the third day, I got the message that I was setting a rotten example for her and about ten days later had quit completely. I knew I needed to give up smoking, but it took the realization of what I was teaching my child to make me do something about it.

In the story of the Prodigal Son told in Luke 15:11-31, the younger of two sons of a wealthy man decided he wanted his inheritance; the father granted his wish, divided his property and gave the younger son his share. The son took what he had been given and went off to a distant country and quickly squandered it on "loose living."

> *When he had freely spent everything, a severe famine struck that country, and he found himself in dire need. So he hired himself out to one of the local citizens who sent him to his farm to tend the swine. And he longed to eat his fill of the pods on which the swine fed, but nobody gave him any. (Luke 15:14-16)*

Saint Luke goes on to say that the son finally "Came to his senses," decided to go back and beg forgiveness and ask his father to make him a hired hand. While humiliated to admit the errors of his ways, at least he would have honest work and food to eat.

The famine is what caused the Prodigal Son to decide to change, the reality that he had nothing left and he was destitute. He had hit such a low rock-bottom that he longed to eat the food given to the pigs he tended. What are the *famines* in our lives that might cause us to initiate change? Could it be that we have found ourselves drinking too much or eating too much or working too much? Could it be that we have fallen into a state of apathy about the practice of our faith? Could it be that our relationship with our spouse is really in a rocky or dangerous place? Could it be we came to the realization the example we are setting for our children or grandchildren is not a positive one? Whatever the case may be, God often sends famines into our lives, not to punish us, but to wake us up or help us recognize our need to change.

Back to the Prodigal Son. As he approached his father's home, his father saw him from a distance, had compassion on him and ran to embrace and kiss him. In spite of the son's pleas to his father to make him a servant, because he was no longer worthy to be called his son, the father set the wheels in motion for a homecoming celebration. Each time we decide to make a positive change, regardless what the change might be, we will experience the very same reception. God will run to us, welcome us back and help us in our efforts through the generous gift of His grace.

The older son was really peeved that his brother would be welcomed back after all he had done. In fact, he said to his father, "Look, in all these years I served you and not once did I disobey your orders; yet you never gave me even a young goat to feast on with my friends. But when your son returns who swallowed up your property with prostitutes, for him you slaughtered the fattened calf." To which the father said, "My son you are here with me always; everything I have is yours. But now we must celebrate and rejoice, because your brother was dead and has come to life again."

Here are a few of the many important messages that can be taken from this parable. First, until I personally choose to make a change, there will be no change. The second is that all reconciliation must be accompanied by commitment to change. A third message, which might be completely overlooked, is that we, like the older son who was obedient to his father, are not being completely open to God's will for us if we simply follow a set of rules, yet allow our hearts to be hard. Instead, we must allow God's grace to work in us so we can grow in love and thus be more like Him.

The "process of change" is far more than just a personal decision to change. Father Cedric Pisegna, in his book, *You Can Change*, points out that once we make our decision, God's grace is what actually empowers us to follow through. Our recognition that we must be more disciplined, for example, about daily exercise or daily prayer is just the first step. We must then ask for God's help to make it happen. So our decision and personal effort, fed by God's grace, is how change actually happens.

Hopefully, by this point in our lives we understand that we do not have the power to change other people. We can, however, help others change by changing the way we respond to them, hoping and praying they will see that change is needed and that they will do what the prodigal son did – admit that he was wrong and get back on the right path.

The next time you are tempted to try to change someone other than yourself, take a hard look in the mirror instead. Remember, in Matthew 7:3, Jesus advises in rather clear language, we should pay more attention to our own faults and do what is necessary to fix ourselves rather than point out and criticize others for their faults:

Why do you look at the speck that is in your brother's eye, but do not notice the log that is in your own eye?

But it is so much easier to judge others and side step our own need for change, isn't it?

As spouses, parents, colleagues and friends we are not disconnected from those around us and their need to change.

In fact, we share a huge responsibility. We exercise that responsibility by modeling behavior that is fully consistent with Scripture, the teachings of the Church, and the laws of our country. We must lead lives fully consistent with principles. For example, we cannot teach our children and grandchildren about honesty, integrity and ethics then do creative or dishonest accounting on our income taxes – even though our children may be totally oblivious to our dishonesty. Or in an even more visible example with our children or grandchildren, fudge the truth about their age when buying movie tickets just so we can save a couple of dollars. If it is okay for us to lie about their age, wouldn't it be okay for them to cheat on a math test? If we cut off another driver in traffic, is that any different than teaching children that it is okay to be rude? And what sort of example are we setting when we spend gracious little time talking or being with them because we are deeply engrossed in cell-phone or ear-bud isolation?

Several years ago I heard an interesting story on National Public Radio. It seems a dad arrived home to find his 8-year old son sitting at the kitchen table working on a poster for school. After the normal affectionate greetings, the dad asked his son if his mom had bought the poster board and markers for him. The boy's sheepish reply was "she bought the poster paper." "Where did you get the markers?" the dad continued. "At school' answered the son, being guarded in his reply. "Oh, I see," said the father, "Your teacher let you bring home the markers, right?" "No, sir," replied his son, even more guarded in his answer than before. "Are you telling me, Son, that you brought these markers home from school without your teacher's permission?" "Yes, sir," responded the son, nearly positive that he was in some serious trouble. With a great deal of indignation, the now angry dad said to his already penitent son, "Don't you ever do that again. If you need markers for a school project call me at work and I will bring them home from the office!"

Let there be no doubt, change does not come easy for most of us, even simple changes. But consider those who have gone through a 12-step process to deal with any sort of substance or alcohol abuse problem, or anyone who struggles to keep their weight in check, or anyone (like me) who commits the same sins time after time. For each, change is hard work. But change can be so much less stressful if we only would look to Scripture, specifically Mark 10:27, where Jesus teaches us:

With people it is impossible, but not with God for all things are possible with God.

Here are some practical steps that I try to keep in mind, when working through change (with no claim as to how effectively I implement them):

- Recognize and admit the need for change. The first step in making change is being truthful about what is going on.
- Ask for God's help. His grace is the driving force behind all positive change.
- Consider sharing your intention with someone, like your spouse or a friend – doing so helps you get support for your change journey.
- Decide what you need to do and set reasonable goals to get there. This helps define your destination and recognizes any substantive change will take time and effort.
- Take ownership of your intention and exercise the discipline to move forward. If your intentions are not personalized they will not get done.
- Take small steps – crawl before you walk, walk before you run, etc.

- Celebrate your progress. We all need a pat on the back from time to time for our hard work.
- Internalize your new habits to the point they begin to feel normal rather than the way they did when you started the change process. Make the change be part of who you are, doing so will then guide what you do.

No matter how difficult change is, we really have no other choice except to embrace it. Change lies between where we are at this moment, and where we want to be. And change is required to cultivate the relationships we have with each other beyond what they are now. Keep in mind reconciliation is one of the highest, most noble forms of change.

All things are possible with God.

Reflection

VII

Celebrating Thanksgiving All Year Long

*Give thanks to the LORD, for he is good, his mercy
endures forever. (Psalm 118:1)*

Just how thankful are you for the gifts God has given you?
Really, how thankful are you? Do you thank Him daily for
those gifts? How about weekly? Ever?

I have been doing some soul-searching recently on the
topic of being thankful for what I have been given. Suppose,
just for a moment, that God began taking away from me
the many things for which I have failed to thank Him.
Fortunately, our loving God is significantly more generous
than any of us, and would not likely take things away from
me just because I did not thank Him for each of those gifts.
But just suppose He did. Which of my limbs and faculties
would be left? Would I still have my hands and my mind?
And what about loved ones? If God were to take away from
me all those persons and things for which I have not given
thanks, what would be left of me?

I have been blessed most of my life with excellent health.
Except for a sickly first grade, and a few minor illnesses and
injuries over my seventy years, I have enjoyed remarkably
good health. Many could likely make the same comment,
but there are those who have had serious health problems,
possibly bordering on death. Several of my buddies have had
heart issues recently, some pretty serious heart issues. I have

personally prayed for many friends and family members during those difficult situations, and then given thanks to God for providing His healing power for their recovery. But in the midst of all those prayers of petition and thanksgiving, I do not remember a single time thanking God for the healthy heart He has given me – very odd and exceedingly presumptuous of me now that I think about it.

Other family members and friends have had serious back and limb ailments, joint replacements, chronic back pain and other sorts of skeletal deteriorations or injuries. While I did amputate a small part of a finger a few years ago, and the injury slowed me down for a while, that small setback was minor compared to some of the issues others have faced and continue to face all the time. How often have I thanked God for the blessing of mobility, physical comfort, and ability to come and go and do virtually anything I need or want to do? In truth, I seldom have. Several years ago, a member of our parish family set a shining example of courage to those of us who knew her. Her daily struggles with the inconceivable challenges she faced because of ALS (Lou Gehrig's disease) were courageous beyond description. In spite of all her physical restrictions, she remained a pillar of strength for those around her. Watching her decline should have been a loud and clear message to me that I should give thanks to God many times each day for the health and strength He has given me. Yet again, I must honestly admit, being thankful for my physical health seldom makes the daily "thank you" prayer list.

Watching family members and others slowly slip away mentally and intellectually because of Alzheimer's or dementia is so very hard. I suspect that most of us take our cognitive abilities and memory for granted – I know I do – even though I watched my wife's mother slip further and further away from us because of advancing dementia. Many have seen parents, in-laws or friends slip away as well. In spite of being around those suffering from such challenges; I can't remember the last time (if ever) I thanked God for whatever mental and intellectual capacities I possess.

When it comes to immediate and extended family, I do a little better, because in our daily prayer time together, my wife and I pray for each member of our family. In my part of our ritual, I give thanks for our children and their spouses, our grandchildren and my siblings and their families; and Laurel gives thanks for her sisters and their families. We pray for each of them, for their health and safety, for God to guide them in all they do each day, that they will be open to the urgings of the Holy Spirit, for God to grant them grace to live righteous lives and for any special intentions that need to be mentioned.

A man's home is his castle. That age-old metaphor could simply mean that the house, condo or apartment where we live is our own personal castle, modest or as grand as it may be, where we rule our kingdom, just as kings did from their castles in days of old. Or it could have a much richer meaning – specifically, that our homes are the place where we can participate in building the kingdom of God. In our homes we live out our royal baptismal kingship and priesthood and serve as prophets to others by cherishing our spouse, raising our children to love and serve God. We influence generations to come when we help our children and grandchildren become true disciples of Jesus. Not sure the last time I specifically thanked Jesus for my home, (or as a dear friend of ours refers to it – The Armbruster Inn) yet I can't think of many places I would rather be than at home.

Throughout my life, I have been blessed with gainful employment, delivering newspapers as a preteen and teen, with the U.S. Geological Survey throughout most of my adult life, and now in post-retirement, in the consulting world. I have taken for granted the education, good fortune, and opportunities afforded me during my entire professional life.

Yet I have seldom specifically thanked God for providing the jobs I needed to pay for college, support my family, and provide for a comfortable retirement. But for the grace of God, I could be on the street, like so many others.

One of the joys of Jesus' life on earth was His relationship with His disciples, particularly the twelve apostles. Jesus was a man just like us, with feelings just like ours. His friends were very special to Him; He loved them dearly. While Scripture does not describe the good times Jesus and His apostles had together, I am positive He enjoyed their companionship. I can see them helping each other in times of need, laughing with each other in times of joy, crying and comforting one another in times of sadness, and experiencing all the other situations and emotions that friends share. Whether in happy times or sad, good times or bad, the relationships we have with friends add significant richness to our lives. We wish them well, we pray for their health and well being, we comfort them. But how often do I consciously thank God for them?

And what about our country? We live in what arguably is the greatest country in the history of the world. The preamble to our Constitution says:

> We the People of the United States, in Order to form a more perfect Union, establish Justice, insure domestic Tranquility, provide for the common defense, promote the general Welfare, and secure the Blessings of Liberty to ourselves and our Posterity, do ordain and establish this Constitution for the United States of America.

Do we generously live up to all of this? The answer is clearly no – we have our problems as a country and as a society. We clearly have more than our share of warts. But for all our problems, for all the things that are not perfect, there are more aspects of our country that are right. As a result, most modern democracies in the world are heavily modeled after ours. How often do I thank God for my wonderful country, despite its imperfections? Not nearly often enough.

In all of what I have mentioned so far, I have suggested the importance of being thankful for what I might call the good things of life – health and happiness, family and friends, our mental capabilities, and our homes and country. I think it is pretty logical that we should be thankful for each of these. But what about times of trial, injuries, illnesses, disappointments, losses of all sorts, etc. Should we also not be thankful for these as well? 1 Thessalonians 5:16-18 says:

*Rejoice always. Pray without ceasing. In **ALL** circumstances give thanks, for this is the will of God for you in Christ Jesus.*

Are we being told to be thankful for our personal bumps in the road and our tragedies? That is exactly what we are being told. Steel is annealed and made stronger by hammering it and gold is refined by fire. Bushes, flowers and fruit bearing plants are more beautiful and fruitful when pruned. Our bodies are made strong when we stress them through exercise. We need to remind ourselves regularly that God never sends us a burden heavier than we are capable of carrying. So is God training us for heavier burdens? We will never really know. However, we are made stronger spiritually, physically, mentally and emotionally by faithfully facing and accepting all that God puts in our path and being thankful to Him for the challenges.

In the Old and New Testaments there are more than one hundred references to the importance of giving thanks. Philippians 4:4-7 says:

Rejoice in the Lord always. I will say it again: Rejoice! Let your gentleness be evident to all. The

Lord is near. Do not be anxious about anything, but in everything, by prayer and petition, with thanksgiving, present your requests to God. And the peace of God, which transcends all understanding, will guard your hearts and your minds in Christ Jesus.

In addition to being thankful for gifts we are given, our petitions should be made with thanksgiving as well. In the Psalms alone there are at least thirty references to praising God through prayers of thanksgiving.

So, here is my prayer of thanksgiving today:

- Thank you, Jesus, for my family, for it is through my relationships with them I begin to experience and understand the depth of the love you have for me.
- Thank you, Jesus, for both my house and my home, for it is there that I experience the love you have for me through my wife, my children and their spouses, my grandchildren, extended family, and friends. For whatever reason, you have allowed me and my family to live there in comfortable and loving surroundings. Please help me to be mindful of and generous to the needs of others less fortunate.
- Thank you, Jesus, for providing meaningful work that allows the opportunity to help others.
- Thank you, Jesus, for the gift of my health. Please help me use my strength for service to you by helping others.
- Thank you, God, for the gift of my mobility, agility and lack of chronic pain. Please help me to use those gifts to help others less fortunate.
- Thank you, Jesus, for the gift of walking, and for the periodic aches and pains and the occasional injury that come from that activity. Help me continue to give you praise with each stride I take and to have a growing appreciation for the suffering of others with any fatigue or discomfort I might feel.

- Thank you, Jesus, for the gift of an intellect that is healthy, curious and seeks to know you better each day. Help me to use the gifts you have given me to help myself and others learn more about you.

- Thank you, Lord, for giving me the gift of friends, who teach me about you, and who help me to appreciate our uniqueness as your children. Please help me to be a model of you to them in all I do and say.

- Thank you, Father, for my country. Help us to be an instrument of your peace in the world by following your ways in all we do.

- And thank you, Jesus, for those times when you send physical, emotion, spiritual or mental challenges to me, because those times require me to have faith in your mercy, kindness and generosity.

- But most of all, dear Father, I thank you for the gifts that I should be most appreciative for every single day of my life, particularly during Lent – the gift of your Son, Jesus, the salvation gift that He gained for me on Good Friday by dying for my sins then rising from the dead on Easter Sunday.

- And, dear Father, if that were not enough, you provided the extraordinary gift of the Holy Eucharist that feeds and nourishes my very soul. To think, each time I receive the Eucharist, I am being given the opportunity to hold the body and blood of Jesus in my hand, then take Him into my body.

- Thank you, Lord. Amen. Amen. Amen.

I can only conclude that I must be far more faithful than I currently am in offering praise and gratitude to God by saying "thank you" to Him. Isn't it odd, how often I say "thank you" to others, even for the smallest of kindnesses, but how infrequently I actually say those words in prayer?

I am continually reminded of the importance and power of Psalm 118:1:

Give thanks to the LORD, for he is good, his mercy endures forever.

Reflection

VIII

Why Do I (We) Question the Will of God?

Before I formed you in the womb I knew you, before you were born I dedicated you, a prophet to the nations I appointed you. (Jeremiah 1:5)

On more than one occasion, I have been bold enough to wonder just what God was thinking when He made certain choices – in short, to question His will. It does not take a lot of Scripture reading or study of history to question why He chose the people He did to do important jobs. Even though the answers may not always be obvious to us, I suspect God smiles from time to time as He looks down on the results of His decisions. Let's look at four examples of what on the surface seem like shaky choices.

The first example is Abraham. When God told Abraham that his elderly, sterile, wife would bear a child in her old age, Abraham laughed – out loud. Then later when Sarah overheard the Lord say she was going to have baby, she laughed as well. The story is recorded in Genesis 17:15-17, 19:

God further said to Abraham: "As for Sarai your wife, do not call her Sarai; her name will be Sarah. I will bless her, and I will give you a son by her. Her also will I bless; she will give rise to nations, and rulers of peoples will issue from her." Abraham fell face down and laughed as he said to himself, "Can

69

a child be born to a man who is a hundred years old? Can Sarah give birth at ninety?" God replied: "Even so, your wife Sarah is to bear you a son, and you shall call him Isaac. It is with him that I will maintain my covenant as an everlasting covenant and with his descendants after him."

Then later, in Genesis 18:1-15:

The LORD appeared to Abraham near the great trees of Mamre while he was sitting at the entrance to his tent in the heat of the day. Abraham looked up and saw three men standing nearby. When he saw them, he hurried from the entrance of his tent to meet them and bowed low to the ground. He said, "If I have found favor in your eyes, my lord, do not pass your servant by. Let a little water be brought, and then you may all wash your feet and rest under this tree. Let me get you something to eat, so you can be refreshed and then go on your way – now that you have come to your servant." "Very well," they answered, "do as you say." So Abraham hurried into the tent to Sarah. "Quick," he said, "get three seahs of fine flour and knead it and bake some bread." Then he ran to the herd and selected a choice, tender calf and gave it to a servant, who hurried to prepare it. He then brought some curds and milk and the calf that had been prepared, and set these before them. While they ate, he stood near them under a tree. "Where is your wife Sarah?" they asked him. "There, in the tent," he said. Then the LORD said, "I will surely return to you about this time next year, and Sarah your wife will have a son." Now Sarah was listening at the entrance to the tent, which was behind him. Abraham and Sarah were already old and well advanced in years, and Sarah was past the age of childbearing. So Sarah laughed to herself as she thought, "After I am worn out and my master is old, will I now have this pleasure?" Then the LORD said to Abraham, "Why did Sarah laugh and say, 'Will I really have a child, now that I am old?' Is anything too hard for the LORD? I will return to you at the appointed time next year and Sarah will have a son." Sarah was afraid, so she lied and said, "I did not laugh." But he said, "Yes, you did laugh."

Isaac got his name from what his parents did. Isaac means "He laughs" or "He will laugh". In the modern world of texting, his name might be abbreviated LOL or "laugh out loud."

Later, as the Lord was getting ready to deal with the debauchery in Sodom, Abraham, who was a faithful servant, pleaded with God on the city's behalf. God said if there were just fifty just people in the city He would spare the city. Abraham went back to the Lord five times getting Him to reduce that number – God finally agreed that if there were five, He would spare the city. As I thought about this, it occurred to me that not long after God performed a miracle and gave Abraham a son, Abraham nagged Him. Remarkable.

God took the old and made them young. Took the sterile and made her fertile. He took the tired and worn and built the foundation for His people. He took the centenarian and made him a negotiator. He took the old and made his descendants as numerous as the grains of sand along the sea.

Many years later, the Israelites were up against a formidable foe in the Philistines. Who could forget the story of David and Goliath? Just imagine the sight – some skinny young kid hops down into a gully with the giant, Goliath, who had just insulted the people of Israel forty days in a row.

71

In your mind, picture this narrative taken from 1 Samuel 17; a few places in the story are comical.

Then Saul dressed David in his own tunic. He put a coat of armor on him and a bronze helmet on his head. David fastened on his sword over the tunic and tried walking around, because he was not used to them. "I cannot go in these," he said to Saul, "because I am not used to them." So he took them off. Then he took his staff in his hand, chose five smooth stones from the stream, put them in the pouch of his shepherd's bag and, with his sling in his hand, approached the Philistine. Meanwhile, the Philistine, with his shield bearer in front of him, kept coming closer to David. He looked David over and saw that he was only a boy, ruddy and handsome, and he despised him. He said to David, "Am I a dog that you come at me with sticks?" And the Philistine cursed David by his gods. "Come here," he said, "and I'll give your flesh to the birds of the air and the beasts of the field!" David said to the Philistine, "You come against me with sword and spear and javelin, but I come against you in the name of the LORD Almighty, the God of the armies of Israel, whom you have defiled. This day the LORD will hand you over to me, and I'll strike you down and cut off your head. Today I will give the carcasses of the Philistine army to the birds of the air and the beasts of the earth, and the whole world will know that there is a God in Israel. All those gathered here will know that it is not by sword or spear that the LORD saves; for the battle is the Lord's, and he will give all of you into our hands.

As the Philistines moved closer to attack him, David ran quickly toward the battle line to meet him.

72

*Reaching into his bag and taking out a stone, he slung
it and struck the Philistine on the forehead. The stone
sank into his forehead, and he fell facedown on the
ground. So David triumphed over the Philistine with
a sling and a stone; without a sword in his hand he
struck down the Philistine and killed him. David ran
and stood over him. He took hold of the Philistine's
sword and drew it from the scabbard. After he killed
him, he cut off his head with the sword.*

As we know, David became the King of all of Israel, the
first person to gather all the tribes together. He was highly
favored by God, handpicked by God to succeed Saul, and
was guided and guarded by God. For much of his life, David
was indeed a man of God's heart, and as Scripture repeats
over and over, the Lord was with David. A large number of
the psalms (at least half) were written by David throughout
his life and are a record of nearly the full range of human
emotions. He was truly inspired by his God and had an
amazing relationship with and faith in Him. Up to this point,
David was God's dedicated servant.

Then one evening, David was taking a stroll on his roof
and just happened to look over the edge and saw Bathsheba
bathing nearby. This man of God should have turned the
other way, but he did not. Instead he had Bathsheba brought
to him, and in his lust took her. After all that God had done to
directly intervene to save and guide David – David slapped
God in the face. Thus was the beginning of his downfall.
Bad went to worse for several decades before David finally
woke up and realized how truly good God had been to him.
Near the end of his life David sang one of the most beautiful
songs in the Old Testament to his God, (2 Samuel 22 and
Psalm 18) thanking Him and asking for forgiveness.

God took His chosen one, David, and made him strong.
Took His favored one and protected and guided him. God

allowed His blessed one the ultimate freedom of choice, knowing that David would sin against Him. He allowed His beloved one to slide down the slippery slope, but before he completely vaporized, God held out His hand and allowed David to grab it. The rise and fall of David should be a remarkable lesson for each of us. We can survive only when we lean on our loving Lord. Why do we choose to do otherwise?

The selection of St. Peter, the rock that God chose to build His church upon, is another choice that seems to violate human logic. Peter was crass, uneducated, often spoke before he thought, and within hours of pledging he would never deny knowing Jesus had done so three times. Does not sound like executive material to me. With candor, however, I must admit the parallels of Peter's weaknesses and my own are frighteningly similar. Peter is often chided for his lack of faith when approaching Jesus on the stormy surface of the Sea of Galilee in the middle of the night, but at least He had the courage to step out of the boat, none of the others did. Yet God smiled on Peter, and just like He did when assuring Abraham and Sarah about Isaac's arrival, asked, "Is there anything that is too hard for God?"

God took the man who denied Him three times and built His church on him. He used the untested one to lead his sheep. He took a man with many shortcomings and provided us an example of how we can and should live. The Lord must still be smiling about how Peter turned out!!

My fourth and final example is one taken from our own time. This man was an ordained minister, had a family, and while deeply revered by many, he was hated and reviled by many others. This man was used to do God's work, but he was a man, with weaknesses, some like those of King David. But each of us is sinful, so it would not be wise to cast stones, would it? This man called our nation's attention to the injustices of racial discrimination. He was the youngest person to ever be awarded the Nobel Prize and was then cut down in the prime of his life by an assassin's bullet. He served as a focal point for calling attention to societal injustice during his lifetime and continues to be a lightning rod even after his death. Martin Luther King, Jr. contributed much by the philosophy of nonviolence he preached, which was quite similar to that espoused by Gandhi years before.

One of King's most famous presentations is often referred to simply as his "I Have a Dream" speech. While all of the speech is not presented here, I would like to share the tail end of it, in hopes that in its reading we will remember the fundamental teachings of Jesus in King's words. They are worth reviewing.

> I have a dream that one day this nation will rise up and live out the true meaning of its creed: "We hold these truths to be self-evident: that all men are created equal."

> I have a dream that one day on the red hills of Georgia the sons of former slaves and the sons of former slave owners will be able to sit down together at the table of brotherhood.

> I have a dream that one day even the state of Mississippi, a state sweltering with the heat of injustice, sweltering with the heat of oppression, will be transformed into an oasis of freedom and justice.

> I have a dream that my four little children will one day live in a nation where they will not be judged by the color of their skin but by the content of their character.

> I have a dream today.

> I have a dream that one day, down in Alabama,

with its vicious racists, with its governor having his lips dripping with the words of interposition and nullification; one day right there in Alabama, little black boys and black girls will be able to join hands with little white boys and white girls as sisters and brothers.

I have a dream today.

I have a dream that one day every valley shall be exalted, every hill and mountain shall be made low, the rough places will be made plain, and the crooked places will be made straight, and the glory of the Lord shall be revealed, and all flesh shall see it together.

This is our hope. This is the faith that I go back to the South with. With this faith we will be able to hew out of the mountain of despair a stone of hope. With this faith we will be able to transform the jangling discords of our nation into a beautiful symphony of brotherhood. With this faith we will be able to work together, to pray together, to struggle together, to go to jail together, to stand up for freedom together, knowing that we will be free one day.

This will be the day when all of God's children will be able to sing with a new meaning, "My country, 'tis of thee, sweet land of liberty, of thee I sing. Land where my fathers died, land of the pilgrim's pride, from every mountainside, let freedom ring."

And if America is to be a great nation this must become true. So let freedom ring from the prodigious hilltops of New Hampshire. Let freedom ring from the mighty mountains of New York. Let freedom ring from the heightening Alleghenies of Pennsylvania!

Let freedom ring from the snowcapped Rockies of Colorado!

Let freedom ring from the curvaceous slopes of California!

But not only that; let freedom ring from Stone Mountain of Georgia!

Let freedom ring from Lookout Mountain of Tennessee!

Let freedom ring from every hill and molehill of Mississippi. From every mountainside, let freedom ring.

And when this happens, when we allow freedom to ring, when we let it ring from every village and every hamlet, from every state and every city, we will be able to speed up that day when all of God's children, black men and white men, Jews and Gentiles, Protestants and Catholics, will be able to join hands and sing in the words of the old Negro spiritual, "Free at last! free at last! thank God Almighty, we are free at last!"

God takes the crooked and makes it straight.

He takes the small and makes them tall.

He takes the chosen and loves us so much He allows us to fall.

So with all this history, why do we continue to question the will of God? He has a plan for each of us, and only us. "God has created me to do Him some definite service. He has committed some work to me which He has not committed to another. I have my mission."

Reflection

Being Good Stewards of Our Gifts

*Much will be required of the person entrusted with
much, and still more will be demanded of the person
entrusted with more. (Luke 6:38)*

Just two weeks after being selected Pope, Francis I challenged
each one of the more than one billion Catholics worldwide to
"Always step outside yourself." In doing so, the Pope added
power to the calls issued by his two predecessors Saint John
Paul II and Pope Emeritus Benedict XVI to actively and
courageously go beyond our comfort zone in spreading the
faith.

The most significant act of faith by anyone in human
history, aside from those taken by Jesus Himself, was the
Virgin Mary's acceptance of God's call to be the mother of
His beloved Son, Jesus. Luke 1:28 says:

*And coming to her, he said, "Hail, favored one! The
Lord is with you."*

As overwhelmed as Mary must have felt, her "Yes" to God's
request, allowed God to pour His divinity into our humanity.

Have you ever been selected for a task that you felt
intimidated by or unequipped to fulfill – like writing a
book, giving a talk on stewardship, visiting the poor in their
homes? Maybe you were asked to lead or participate in a
ministry in your parish that seemed beyond your reach. Or

perhaps you were faced with something quite unexpected like dealing with a significant health issue or the special needs of a child or an elderly parent who requires constant care. Perhaps you were surprised that you were called, or felt that surely someone else was more qualified. Those times can be quite daunting.

As difficult as such challenges can be, we must keep in mind that when God chooses us, He also equips us. He never fails to give us all the grace we need to carry out His call. Even the apostles had their moments of doubt and confusion. But at Pentecost, when they received the outpouring of the Holy Spirit, they were filled with the power they needed to preach the good news. And look at what they accomplished: more than three thousand were baptized following Peter's first sermon!

If you are feeling overwhelmed by what God is asking you to do, step back and breathe slowly and deeply. Think about the apostles and the day of Pentecost. Think, too, about Mary and the way she surrendered to God's call. Most importantly, ask the Holy Spirit to give you greater confidence because of His presence. The Holy Spirit loves it when we turn to Him, and is more than happy to give us all we need to carry out our calling.

So what does all this have to do with stewardship? Stewardship is all about the way we respond to God's call in our lives. It is defined by our spirituality. Stewardship is fulfilling the baptismal obligations of priest, prophet and king. How do I share the gifts God has given me? How do I use my time each day? How do I give my financial resources to support the Church and those in need? All of these are tough questions requiring much thought before answering.

Typically, when the topic of stewardship is discussed, the three T's mentioned are time, talent, and treasure. Yet many people hear only *treasure* and immediately think, "Oh great, here comes the request for money." We would do well to just let our blood pressure settle down a bit! Consider that stewardship is simply the offering of our entire selves to God. We have the choice to live self-centered lives, or Christ-centered lives. Knowing that God gives us all our time, talent and treasure, does it not seem logical that we should return to Him the first fruits of these gifts.

In the opening words of their pastoral letter on Stewardship in 2013, the U.S. Catholic Bishops said, "Once one chooses to become a disciple of Jesus Christ, stewardship is not an option." The bishops further instruct, "As Christian stewards, we (must) receive God's gifts gratefully, cultivate them responsibly, share them lovingly in justice with others, and return them with increase to the Lord."

One measure of giving is a term that causes many to shudder – *tithing*. A brief but beautiful story from Mark 12:42-44 provides useful insight into what it means to give sacrificially:

> *A poor widow came and put in two small coins, the equivalent of a penny. Then he called his disciples and said to them, "In truth I tell you, this poor widow has put in more in than all who have contributed to the treasury; for they have all put in money they could spare, but she in her poverty has put in everything she possessed, all she had to live on."*

Are we called to abandon everything we have, like St. Francis of Assisi did? Not necessarily. But we are called to give of ourselves as the widow did, to give from our livelihood, which could be in the form of our time, our talent or our treasure. Regardless, tithing is giving up, giving to, and giving of one's heart. It is a priceless labor of love.

In Luke 6:38 Jesus tells us:

Give and gifts will be given to you; a good measure,
packed together, shaken down, and overflowing, will
be poured into your lap. For the measure with which
you measure will in return be measured out to you.

But tithing also applies to the generous giving of both our time and talent. When tithing our time, just like with tithing our financial resources, we are asked to give 10% to God. Ten percent of twenty-four hours is two hours and twenty-four minutes a day. Sounds like a lot, doesn't it? For those who believe tithing of our income means 10% after taxes, they would likely say something like, "but I sleep eight hours a day, so shouldn't I get a break and only have to give one hour and thirty-six minutes to God?" I'm not going to get into that debate. Regardless of whether we give two hours and twenty-four minutes or one hour and thirty-six minutes per day, it is still a lot of time. There are many ways we can give our time in service and dedication to the Lord – including praying, reading or studying Scripture, meditating, or visiting the sick, helping a neighbor or volunteering our time to a ministry that helps the poor like St. Vincent de Paul, Catholic Charities or Habitat for Humanity. For many, particularly parents of young children, finding blocks of time for prayer, scripture reading, etc., can, frankly be a real challenge. But, that being said, the opening Mass prayer (Collect) for the twentieth Sunday in Ordinary time should offer us some consolation:

O God, who have prepared for those who love you good things which no eye can see, fill our hearts, we pray, with the warmth of your love, so that, *loving you in all things and above all things*, we may attain your promises, which surpass every human desire. Through our Lord Jesus Christ, your Son, who lives and reigns with you in the unity of the Holy Spirit, one God, for ever and ever.

Loving you in all things and above all things... Might want to do an inventory and assess where you are. If you are short on the time you give God, like I am, start trying to add some small manageable increments.

What about tithing our talent? Giving what constitutes a tenth of our talent is not as easy as with time and money. Actually, tithing our talent means that we must be willing to offer the very best talents we have, our first fruits. It might be done by joining the choir and sharing the voice God gave you. But if you are able to use your spirituality, insight and religious education to teach a CCD (or Sunday school) class, then maybe it is time to consider stepping up to the plate. There are lots of opportunities here.

In Luke 12:48 Our Lord lovingly advises us:

Much will be required of the person entrusted with much, and still more will be demanded of the person entrusted with more.

Tithing serves two fundamental purposes. First it supports the Church, but second and more importantly, a tithe is a symbolic gesture that recognizes the reality that all we have in this world really belongs to God. To show us the way, God the Father gave us His first fruit, His Son, to replace the Old Testament sacrifices by Jesus' dying on the Cross. We imitate the Father's love for us by giving to Him the best we have to offer.

If a man showers his wife with gifts but does not love her, his gestures are empty. If the wife loves the gifts more than her husband, her actions are equally empty. Giving God our skill and wealth without giving of our self is meaningless. Tithing our treasure, without giving God our talent, and perhaps more valuable, our time, is empty, just like the husband who gives his wife lavish gifts but never spends time with her. To put a strong exclamation point on the importance of giving time, we would do well to consider that *time* is the very first of God's creation. If that sounds contrary to your understanding of the creation story in Genesis 1, just recall that the first three words of the bible are "In the beginning..." Before God decided to create the heavens and the earth, he created time! Stewardship has the power to shape and mold our understanding of our lives and the way we live.

As reinforcement, we are cautioned in James 2:26:

> *For just as a body without a spirit is dead, so also faith without works is dead.*

At times, we find it far too easy to ignore spiritual realities and to deny that religion must play a fundamental role in shaping human and social values. While our relationship with God is a very private matter, the practice of our religion is anything but private. As Catholics we live in the mainstream of American society and experience many of its advantages, but it is also a secular society that bombards us with temptations, that adversely influence what we think, say and do. Accepting the challenge of Christian stewardship, rather than giving in to the temptations of self-centeredness and greed can be quite overwhelming. Therefore, we must make extraordinary efforts to understand the true meaning of stewardship and live accordingly. Each member of the Church has her or his own special God-given role to play. Once we choose to become a disciple of Jesus Christ, stewardship is not an option. How will I answer the call? Will I personally accept the challenges issued by our current and two former Popes and "always step outside myself?" I certainly hope and pray so.

Reflection

X

Be a Positive Role Model – Encourage Others

*For I have set you an example, that you also should
do as I have done to you. (John 13:15)*

Many of you reading this reflection may go to daily mass
and are quite tuned in to the cycle of feast days the Church
celebrates. Others, like me, might not be so sharply focused.
Did you know that we celebrate the feast of St. Joseph on June
11? Surely a few eyebrows are twitching – some are thinking
the feast of St. Joseph is celebrated on March 19. A few more
scholarly types may have a "you must be mistaken" look on
your face, "June 11 is the feast of St. Barnabas, one of the
early disciples of the church." Well, truth be told, whichever
group you were in (unless you didn't have a clue), your
answer was correct. The feast of Jesus' earthly father, St.
Joseph, is celebrated on March 19, and June 11 is the feast
of St. Barnabas.

But no doubt some of you biblical scholars know that
Barnabas was not the name his parents gave him. In fact,
Joseph was Barnabas' birth name – that's right, Joseph. His
disciple buddies named him Barnabas, and for good reason.
Acts 4:32-36 says:

*The community of believers was of one heart and one
mind, and no one claimed that any of his possessions
was his own, but they had everything in common.
With great power the apostles bore witness to the*

resurrection of the Lord Jesus, and great favor was accorded them all. There was no needy person among them, for those who owned property or houses would sell them, bring the proceeds of the sale, and put them at the feet of the apostles, and they were distributed to each according to need. Thus Joseph, also named by the apostles Barnabas (which is translated "son of encouragement"), a Levite, a Cypriot by birth, sold a piece of property that he owned, then brought the money and put it at the feet of the apostles.

Joseph – Barnabas – *Son of Encouragement* – what an interesting and fascinating sequence of names for a guy the people of Lystra called, *Zeus,* because they thought he was a god who had come to them in human form. That same group of people called Paul, *Hermes,* son of *Zeus.* But Barnabas was only a man – a very humble and holy man – dedicated to helping others come to know the Lord Jesus Christ. So how could there have been so much confusion and why do we not know more about Barnabas?

Many of you are sports fans, each with your favorite sport(s) and I suspect most of you have favorite players or sports figures. But how many great baseball, football, basketball players or how many great golfers are hardly known because they played in the shadow of legends like Babe Ruth, Joe DiMaggio, Mickey Mantle, Michael Jordan, Johnny Unitas, or Jack Nicklaus and Arnold Palmer? How many great artists and musicians found themselves living in the shadow of the greats of their day, such as Andrea del Sarto and Antonio Solieri? It is really tough to get much sun on you when you are contemporaries with the likes of Michelangelo or Wolfgang Amadeus Mozart. Yet in every field, some of the finest practitioners who ever competed, performed, designed or produced fine art became footnotes (or practically footnoted) in history. Had they been born or shared their gifts at any other time, they, too, would have gotten top billing as being among the most influential in their trade.

On a very different scale, during his senior year at St. Pius, my son, David, claimed that he played on the "second best high school soccer team" in the State of Georgia. Yes, he was on the varsity team that won the state championship that year, but he got little time on the field during games. He was on the second squad, the one the first team scrimmaged against every day in practice, always holding their own against the starters, and frequently getting the best of them. Even though his squad got little outward recognition by being given field time during varsity games, they were part of the crew who sport the State Championship ring that to him is still a reminder of his hard work and dedication. He was a really a fine soccer player who played in the shadow of others.

Similarly, those who love mystery novels know that overlooked, but ever-present seemingly minor details are often the key to solving the crime. Some of the best who-done-it series on television over the last several decades have taken advantage of this ploy as well.

But let's be realistic. Barnabas' name does not conger up the same level of recognition as his contemporaries such as Peter, Paul, John, Mark, Matthew and others. Yet, Barnabas is a huge figure in the establishment of the early church. He was a key player in numerous critical events in those decades immediately following the death and resurrection of Jesus. For example, Barnabas went to Antioch from Jerusalem to encourage the believers there when they were struggling. You may recall the first community to be referred to as Christians was in Antioch. In Acts 11:23-24, Luke tells us:

When he arrived and saw the grace of God, he rejoiced and encouraged them all to remain faithful to the Lord in firmness of heart, for he was a good man, filled with the Holy Spirit and faith. And a large number of people was added to the Lord.

Barnabas was the one who personally traveled to Tarsus to look for Paul, and when he found him brought him to Antioch. In fact, when we read about Paul's adventures throughout much of the Acts of the Apostles, Barnabas was at Paul's side, often one of those overlooked details – Paul getting much attention for his preaching, while Barnabas waited in the wings. But in Antioch, it was Barnabas' gift of gentle persuasion at work in the background that helped unravel the long standing animosity between the Jews and Gentiles there and bridged the gap between those groups.

A meditation published in *The Word Among Us* on the feast of St. Barnabas a couple of years ago, observed:

Without Barnabas, Paul may have remained an overzealous convert in faraway Tarsus. It was Barnabas who first convinced the apostles to accept Paul after his conversion. It was Barnabas who brought Paul to Antioch, enlisting his help and placing him in his first leadership role. The two traveled together, evangelizing, establishing churches, braving persecutions and working out what it meant to be a disciple in the pagan world outside Jerusalem.

Barnabas was an extremely generous man, giving all of his personal wealth to the church, much of it to help the poor in the original church in Jerusalem. He was the one who gave John Mark a second chance when Paul was ready to pull the plug on him. The fifteenth chapter of Acts says rather clearly, that Paul wanted little else to do with John Mark after a few indiscretions. Barnabas' willingness to keep the faith with John Mark proved to be a wise and virtuous thing to do, because John Mark himself later became very influential in the early church. What remarkable outcomes from the loving patience of one whose ministry was lived in the shadow of others.

There are modern day examples of similar outcomes of encouragement. For managers, parents or grandparents, or role models (that includes all of us), the most important lesson is simple – whenever helping others, remove your ego and personal gain from the equation. Each of us has opportunities to influence the lives of others, frankly more than we will ever know, but we do not need to get credit. We simply need to serve, then get out of the way and allow sun to shine on others, for their accomplishments. As a parent, work hard to set a good example for your children, watch them excel, and even though you are "busting your buttons" proud of them, allow their accomplishments to speak for themselves, taking no credit personally for what they have done on their own. Avoid having the light shine on you. As a manager or supervisor, identify someone with potential, challenge and assist them to grow exponentially by mentoring or giving them opportunities, then let them soar. Maybe the person you help develop along the way will later become your boss and/or mentor. What a wonderful gift. What a wonderful reward for your soul.

The composer of one of my favorite contemporary songs is an example of a person who has spent his life making other musicians and vocalists famous. His name is David Foster. The song, *The Prayer*, Foster wrote originally for Celine Dion. He is the person who discovered her when she was just eighteen. My favorite version of the song, however, is one recorded by Andre Bochelli and Katherine McPhee. Many of the beautiful recordings Bochelli has made in his career were written or produced by Foster, and the career of McPhee has skyrocketed because of Foster's recognition and promotion of her superb talent. Foster is also the guy who discovered Josh Groben, and produced his famous song *You*

Lift Me Up. He wrote, produced or promoted for the likes of Peter Cetera, Michael Buble', Bozz Skaggs and many other well known artists. Foster has a forty-year track record of finding, encouraging, and developing others. Sure he gets a great deal of attention, but he is likely better known as a master of encouragement of the work of others.

A dear priest friend, Father Larry McNeil, an adopted member of our family, is another one of those people who so generously uses his gifts to influence and encourage others. For nearly forty years he has been part of our family. He has prayed with and for us, has been with us during joyous and difficult times, has weathered times of tough decisions with us, been godfather to our son, been official Church witness at both of our children's weddings and baptized two of our three grandchildren. During tough times, he simply has the gift to know what to say, and when to say it. And while we have told him many times how much he means to each of us, and he knows it to be so, he surely does not know just how much influence he has had on our family, and beyond. We, like so many others, are blessed to have him in our lives.

Few of us get the opportunity to perform or be recognized on an international stage in any field of endeavor. Yet, the most influential people in my own life, and I strongly suspect in yours, were not individuals who got much recognition beyond a very small sphere of influence. Most of us are not likely to make the world stage, unless "world" is defined more narrowly as extending to just beyond those whom we influence directly, that is our family, friends, colleagues, neighbors, and maybe only one level of influence beyond them.

Yes, Joseph's colleagues nicknamed him Barnabas (remember – son of encouragement), but not because they thought him to be influential on the world stage. Rather they saw him as a man of godly character and knew him to be dedicated, just, generous, and steadfast in his love of

Jesus. Barnabas desperately wanted others to love Him, too. Barnabas lived the very virtues Jesus taught and in so doing those coming to the faith felt warmly welcomed.

I mentioned briefly that Barnabas was the one who went to Tarsus and brought the newly converted Saul, now Paul, out into the world. Had that one invitation not been issued – an invitation clearly inspired by the Holy Spirit working through Barnabas – the course of history might have played out quite differently than it has. Cardinal Newman's prayer, "The Mission of My Life," emphasizes that each of us is "a link in a chain, a bond of connection between persons." Barnabas was a critical link in a very important chain of relationships.

Most of us do not realize the huge importance of the small things we say or do. An encouraging word to someone may be what saves that person from taking his or her own life or the life of another. One act of kindness may bring a spark of hope that encourages a loved one or colleague to try again and again. The demonstration of love to a perfect stranger may show that person that she or he has value – something that may have been forgotten because of all that life has thrown at them. Taking a chance on someone, when logic says that doing so is a bad idea, might make the difference in whether someone lives their life motivated or takes the opposite route.

A popular Catholic author and speaker, Matthew Kelly, in his book, *Perfectly Yourself,* observes that no one can ever become the best version of himself if the first question he asks in most situations is, "What's in it for me." We can only become the best versions of ourselves – the one God created us to be – when our first question in any situation is "How can I serve." I have shared this observation recently with two different cadres of clients and several one-on-one coaching clients with remarkable reactions. In each case, when looking at their individual and collective faces, it was like a flood light turned on. That we (I) must be about serving others rather than ourselves, sounds a resilient chord.

We have often heard and maybe even often used the expression "There, but through the grace of God, go I" when observing the plight of others less fortunate than ourselves. What a wonderful way of recognizing the gifts God gives us, even when we do not deserve them. Barnabas lived out the missionary role God created for him. He did not complain, he simply accepted many colossal challenges, and in doing so he directly encouraged thousands in the early church and, maybe, indirectly hundreds of millions throughout history. Yet he did little that was special; instead he did what Mother Teresa often spoke about – he did many little things with great love.

From the same meditation quoted earlier from *The Word Among Us*,

> In a world that is often hostile or indifferent to the gospel, those who manifest a strong Christian character – even the 'hidden' ones like Barnabas – can play a vital role in evangelizing and in encouraging other believers.

In a talk she gave at a retreat in Las Vegas several years ago, Paula D'Arcy proposed that the expression, "There but through the grace of God, go I," be rearranged as a different and very proactive challenge about how we should live our lives. "There with the grace of God, I will go." Such a change is in keeping with the example set by St. Barnabas. Think about it. "There with the grace of God, I will go." God gives us His grace, we accept it, then with His grace we become the best versions of who He created us to be. Regardless the situation, our first order of business should never be about wanting to know what we will receive in return for our action, instead our attention needs to be focused on how we can serve those around us. Newman offers:

> I shall do good, I shall do His work. I shall be an angel of peace, a preacher of truth in my own place, while not intending it, if I do but keep His commandments.

The Greek philosopher Heraclitus once wrote, "The content of your character is your choice. Day by day, what you choose, what you think, and what you do is who you become." We have so many opportunities to choose how we live our lives – supporting others, offering a smile or a kind word or a helping hand, recognizing the potential in others and helping them achieve the best version of themselves, living lives of service – each of these are different ways of using the grace God gives us each day, encouraging others along the way.

How will you humbly serve today in your own place? How will you be a Barnabas?

Reflection

XI

Living with Today's Realities

⚬⚬⚬

Let every person be subordinate to the higher
authorities, for there is no authority except from God,
and those that exist have been established by God.
(Romans 13:1)

In the weeks following the election of our current (44th) president, I spent a great deal of time reflecting on today's realities. Our country had just elected a new commander-in-chief who, in my opinion, would very likely make significant changes that could challenge the very moral framework upon which our country was founded, a framework that should govern each of our lives. For several months leading up to this election my wife and I prayed the rosary daily that God would guide our nation's electorate. And now, the candidate who had pledged his first act as president would be to push for the passage of the Freedom of Choice Act had been elected – surprisingly enough with millions of votes from those professing the same religious affiliation as we. We felt abandoned and disheartened. We questioned the will of God in this situation. And we felt deep concern about the tragedy of the millions of unborn children that could be murdered, before or immediately after, they draw their first breath as a direct result of the Freedom of Choice Act, which would take Roe v. Wade to a very different, very unsettling plane.

On the morning after Election Day, in a time of genuine frustration and concern, we set about our normal early morning devotion routine, which includes the Scripture readings for daily Mass and a meditation on those readings taken from a Catholic periodical, *The Word Among Us*. As so often happens, the message that we both most needed to hear in that moment was there waiting for us.

The gospel reading for the day was Luke 14: 25-33, a message clearly defining discipleship and what it means to be a true follower of Christ – a message remarkably on target, from our perspective for the situation of the day. The Psalm reading included 27:1-4 and 13-14:

"The Lord is my light and my salvation; whom do I fear? The Lord is my life's refuge, of whom should I be afraid? When evildoers come at me to devour my flesh, my enemies and foes themselves stumble and fall. Though an army encamp against me, my heart does not fear; though war be waged against me, even then do I trust. One thing I ask of the Lord; this I seek: to dwell in the Lord's house all the days of my life. To gaze on the Lord's beauty, to visit his temple."

I believe I shall enjoy the Lord's goodness in the land of the living. Wait for the Lord, take courage; be stouthearted, wait for the Lord!

What a wonderfully comforting message to hear in this time of disappointment and genuine concern about the future of our children and grandchildren, our society, our country.

But the message from the epistle for that same day was possibly even more relevant and to the point. It was taken from Paul's letter to his beloved Philippians 2:12-18, (this paragraph is entitled, *Obedience and Service in the World*) – only part of the reading 2:14-16 is presented here):

"So then my brothers, obedient as you have always been, not only when I am present but all the more now

*when I am absent, work out your salvation with fear
and trembling. For God is the one who, for his good
purpose, works in you both to desire and to work. Do
everything without grumbling or questioning, that
you may be blameless in the midst of a crooked and
perverse generation, among whom you shine like
lights in the world, as you hold on to the word of life,
so that my boast for the day of Christ may be that I
did not run in vain or labor in vain."*

From the daily meditation in *The Word Among Us* I found
many take-away insights. For example, we all know people
who seldom, if ever, lose their cool despite what life throws at
them. They keep a peaceful demeanor, keep a warm smile on
their faces, and always seem to have a kind word. Wouldn't
it be frustrating if we constantly compared ourselves to folks
like this, especially if we tend to have a short fuse? Wouldn't
it be nice to absorb just a small dose of their serenity? But if
we would simply remember that God loves us just the way
we are, we would find more internal peace and significantly
greater hope. Keep in mind that "God loves a cheerful giver"
(2 Corinthians 9:7). Whenever we serve the Lord and others
with joy, and avoid boastfulness, we bring glory to the Lord.
So how can we do better? By insuring our perspective and
energy is pointed in the right direction. Rather than focusing
on the difficult task at hand and thinking it's all up to us,
we should always keep in mind that Christ provides our
hope of glory. He is our hope for peace and surrender. Jesus
will never let us be tried beyond our strength (1 Corinthians
10:13) – even when we feel weak or abandoned.

We are facing a serious moral crisis in our country today
and frankly, it is pushing me and many of the people I know
to our limit and some to near despair. But our human limit
is the place where God works most effectively in our lives.
Because we like to be in control of our surroundings, and we

now feel pretty helpless, God may be using this situation to draw us closer to Him. If we are tempted to give up at the first sign of trouble, God may be trying to give us greater confidence in His love and His power. Wherever we might be individually or collectively, we must keep our eyes fixed on Jesus. Our circumstances may not change, but our hearts surely will! Presidents come and go, governments come and go, crises come and go. But God is always there, is always on our side, and He always has our welfare as His priority. If we place our faith in Him, we will survive – and prosper. And as if the meditation was not comforting enough, the final prayer was truly consoling:

> Lord, we know that you can handle every situation that life throws at us. So we offer our whole life to you. Fill us with your Spirit, and transform us with your joy!

We looked at each other in amazement, raised our eyes to heaven and at the same time said, "Thank you, Jesus, we needed to hear all of that."

As I thought more about the election results, the scripture passages for the day after the election, my thoughts and concerns (and frankly fears about the future of our country and way of life), I realized that if I really do have faith in Jesus, I have to accept that all good things come to those who believe. I must hold fast to the knowledge that God will keep His promise to us, that He will not abandon us or forget us, and that His plans are for our good, not our demise. Sounds easy, doesn't it? But staying positive in a time of great torment is tough, really tough, because so often we are far too self-reliant, falling into the trap of we must know more, understand more – in short, be in control of our destinies. But Jesus asks us to put our hope and trust in Him.

Do we have the courage and faith to do that? Do I have the courage and faith to do that?

St. Paul wrote to the people of the newly formed Church that was founded during the pagan brutality of the imperial Roman Empire. Our situation today might actually pale by comparison. In Paul's letter to Titus, Paul reminds us that we have an obligation to be obedient to civil authorities (so long as doing so does not violate the law of God) and to be open to all good enterprise, regardless of its origin. He says further we must not slander anyone, must be peaceable, considerate and gracious to everyone. While we live in a very different society than Paul, nonetheless, we are in a really challenging time. Paul knew from personal experience about corrupt officials, so his advice was written to members of the Christian church rather than government officials. Paul's letter to Titus 3:1-7, provides marvelous insight and guidance for us today:

> *Remind them to be under the control of magistrates and authorities, to be obedient, to be open to every good enterprise. They are to slander no one, to be peaceable, considerate, exercising all graciousness toward everyone. For we ourselves were once foolish, disobedient, deluded, slaves to various desires and pleasures, living in malice and envy, hateful ourselves and hating one another. But when the kindness and generous love of God our savior appeared, not because of any righteous deeds we had done but because of his mercy, he saved us through the bath of rebirth and renewal by the Holy Spirit, whom he richly poured out on us through Jesus Christ our savior, so that we might be justified by his grace and become heirs in hope of eternal life.*

The meditation on this reading from *The Word Among Us* was also brilliantly spot on:

> Without sacrificing truthfulness, we are to slander no one but to look for the good in everyone. We are to encourage "every good enterprise" that makes life better for humankind, no matter whose idea it was or what motive they may have had in suggesting it. But it's not enough just to be good, obedient citizens. As temples of the Holy Spirit, we have much to offer, both in our political process and in our neighborhoods. God calls us to work actively for peace and reconciliation among people of different backgrounds and opinions. He calls us, too, to be gracious and considerate toward everyone, especially those whom society may consider disposable or worthless.

Paul told Timothy (1 Tim 2:1-2), we are to pray diligently for those who lead our national and local governments, even if they do not acknowledge God's authority. Their authority still comes from God, and God can use them to advance His purposes. Just as we need to be the sources of blessing and inspiration to those who lead us, those who lead us must truly dedicate themselves to the common good.

What does all of this mean in the context of decisions being made by our president and other elected officials? Very simply, we must remain ever vigilant of what goes on in our political processes, particularly related to our beliefs and responsibilities as Catholics, as Christians, as people of good will. Issues related to the sanctity of life at all stages of development should be of particular concern. For example, we should steadfastly insist on safeguarding the standing executive order banning embryonic stem cell research, despite efforts to legalize that research. Rather than sitting idly by, we need to express our opinions loudly and often on such issues to White House comment lines and to our entire Congressional delegation – regardless of political party affiliation. I have not done nearly enough pushing back in the past, and I need to be far more active going forward.

As Catholics, as Christians of all denominations, we need to courageously stand up for and be vocal about our beliefs on a wide range of issues, but especially about the sanctity of life, because if we fail there, countless lives will continue to be snuffed out before they have a chance. Archbishop Wilton Gregory of Atlanta, Georgia, in his pre-election message to the Archdiocese in 2007, counseling the faithful about our voting responsibilities as Catholics, used the words from our Nation's Declaration of Independence, "Life, liberty and the pursuit of happiness." His point was that even our nation's founding fathers used "Life" as the first and most prominent reason to pursue our independence. We must make our voices heard. "Without life, the rest is simply details."

In addition, and likely more important than any other thing we can do, including responsibly pushing back on every occasion and in every situation when we believe we are being drawn away from what God wants of us, is to pray. The power of prayer is limitless. So, prayer warriors, let's get rolling.

O God, we live in a political reality that often seems far removed from your kingdom. Bless those who lead our country. Correct their errors, and strengthen every good impulse.

Reflection

Jesus is the Model Servant

*Blessed are those servants whom the master finds
vigilant on his arrival. Amen I say to you, he will gird
himself, have them recline at table, and proceed to
wait on them. (Luke 12:37)*

One of the true blessings of our Catholic faith tradition is the
3-year cycle for Sundays and 2-year cycle of daily scripture
readings used at mass. Those cycles include the essence of
both the Old and New Testaments spread over three years.
Because my wife and I try to read the daily passages together
each day, they frequently serve as stimulation for reflections
I have written over the years.

A recent Gospel passage struck a resounding chord for
me and was the source of inspiration for this particular
reflection. The message brings into clear focus many parts
of our faith journey and relationship with God – or at least
it should. I must admit, however, I did not connect all of the
dots at first. The passage is Luke 12:35-38:

*Gird your loins and light your lamps and be like
servants who await their master's return from a
wedding, ready to open immediately when he comes
and knocks. Blessed are those servants whom the
master finds vigilant on his arrival. Amen, I say to
you, he will gird himself, have them recline at table,
and proceed to wait on them. And should he come in*

*the second or third watch and find them prepared in
this way, blessed are those servants.*

In many of the stories in Holy Scripture, particularly the
parables told by Jesus to His disciples, the bridegroom, the
master of the house, etc. comes home late, and the servants
"jump to" to do their servant duties. This story is different.

In the meditation on this reading in *The Word Among Us*
that my wife and I use each morning along with the daily mass
readings, there were some marvelous observations about this
four-verse gospel, that frankly, I had not considered. Quoting
from the meditation:

> What a reversal! First, Jesus tells His disciples
> to be vigilant and to work hard, always ready for
> His return. But then, He tells them that if He finds
> them hard at work, He will have them recline at
> table, and proceed to wait on them. Why such royal
> treatment (for the servants)? Wouldn't you expect
> Him instead to acknowledge their dedication, and
> then encourage them to keep up the good work?

> What is most amazing in this parable is the image
> about who it is who will be serving us. It is Jesus
> Christ, the eternal Son of God! Imagine that He, the
> Holy One of Israel, the Alpha and the Omega, will
> become a servant and tend to our needs!

But we really should not be surprised that the Holy One
of Israel would stoop to be our servant. We are told in Saint
Paul's letter to the Philippians 2:3-8 (one of my favorite
passages in the Bible) that we should:

> *Do nothing out of selfishness or out of vainglory; rather
> humbly regard others as more important than yourselves,
> each looking out not for his own interests but also for*

*those of others. Have among yourselves the same attitude
that is also yours in Christ Jesus, who, though he was
in the form of God, did not regard equality with God,
something to be grasped. Rather, he emptied himself,
taking the form of a slave, coming in human likeness,
and found human in appearance, he humbled himself,
becoming obedient to death, even death on a cross.*

What a remarkable statement about Jesus' love for us. He
became a slave. He washed the feet of His disciples. He knelt
down in front of us and washed away all of our sins. And equally
amazing, after doing all of that, He clothed us with a dignity
that we do not deserve and sits us down to a lavish feast. How
absolutely remarkable! Our God is an awesome God.

Even though the story of the Last Supper is very familiar,
I find it useful to remind myself of that story regularly. The
part that always deeply touches my heart is John 13:6-10:

*He came to Simon Peter, who said to him, "Master
are you going to wash my feet?" Jesus answered
and said to him, "What I am doing, you do not
understand now, but you will understand later."
Peter said to him, "You will never wash my feet."
Jesus answered him, "Unless I wash you, you will
have no inheritance with me." Simon Peter said to
him, "Master, then not only my feet, but my hands
and head as well." Jesus said to him, "Whoever has
bathed has no need except to have his feet washed,
for he is clean all over; so you are clean.*

You just gotta love Peter. At first he wants nothing to do with
having Jesus wash his feet; then, when he finally catches
on he wants to be bathed all over. Aren't we sometimes just
like Peter? I certainly am – frequently trying to second guess
God. Why not simply listen to the Lord's instructions – then
follow them? Jesus is the humble servant, who shows us

the way. According to Scott Hahn, professor of theology at Franciscan University, humility is "loving service to others." Would it not be easier for us to simply follow the guidance Jesus provides?

At our home parish, our congregation has been blessed to experience our pastor's personal example of humble service in the way he washes feet as part of the liturgy on Holy Thursday evening. As most ministers do, he washes and dries the person's foot, only then he very reverently bends down and tenderly kisses their foot then warmly embraces them. The first time I saw that loving act, I was (and frankly still am) deeply moved, both emotionally and spiritually. What a beautiful and moving experience.

In the story of the Prodigal Son, the father, in the true spirit of being a servant, lovingly clothed his wayward son in a new robe when he returned home, a symbol of his restored dignity, and then sat a feast before him – a celebration of the lost being found. But there is another part of the Prodigal Son narrative that I would like to draw attention to here, that I have not heard about before. The last time I heard a homily on this story, I was with some Catholic friends and former colleagues at a meeting in Denver. Together we attended Sunday mass at a nearby Catholic church. After the deacon had read the very familiar passage, the celebrant walked to the pulpit and commented, almost in despair, "How do you preach a homily about one of the most magnificent stories in the New Testament?" He then went on to preach an absolutely extraordinary sermon centered on a *single word* from the story of the prodigal son. Luke 15:20 says:

> *While he was still a long way off, his father caught sight of him, and was filled with **compassion**. He ran to his son, embraced him and kissed him.*

The word that is vitally important in this passage and the single word the entire sermon focused on was

COMPASSION. As so often happens when scripture is translated from an ancient language such as Hebrew, Greek or Latin, much can be lost, in spite of the biblical scholars' best efforts to translate accurately. The English language has significant limitations – and this is one of those cases. If I remember correctly what the celebrant said, there are at least six Hebrew words for our English word *compassion*. In the Hebrew text of this story, the word 'compassion' is *rachamim* (emphasis on the *ha*), a word that loosely translates as "mother love," the kind of love a mother has for the unborn child in her womb, the kind of love that can at the same time hurt deeply and be joyful and wondrous. He pointed out that one does not have to be a woman to feel this form of compassion. The prodigal son probably did not deserve *rachamim*, but the father, without question, was overjoyed to see his son's return. Would any of us as parents welcome a prodigal daughter or son back in the way this father did, and as our loving God does us when we stray? Hopefully we would. Almost surely we would. Or would we?

Even though this explanation of *rachamim* is rudimentary at best and I suspect most are not familiar with the term, there is so much we can learn. According to the celebrant that day in Denver, as hard as it may be to believe, most of us reject *rachamim* from our loving Father, and at an alarming rate, by refusing to accept our Divine Father's compassionate forgiveness for our transgressions. Our refusal takes many forms, but most are founded in arrogance, self-righteousness, and pride. One small example, and he mentioned several others, is our reluctance to fully confess our sins in confession because we are too proud to admit our indiscretions, or we rationalize and convince ourselves that what we have done is not really sinful, when in fact it is. To receive the gift of *rachamim*, we must humble ourselves before God, tell the truth, and then humbly accept His wonderful forgiveness.

107

The parable of the Prodigal Son tells us a lot about our mission in life. Is it to work ourselves into a frenzy? Or to stay busy just so Jesus will not find us idle when He returns? Surprisingly, it is neither. Our mission is to serve one another with love, just as Jesus served us with love – not with full-time, full-on intensity, rather with patience, dedication and perseverance. In much the same way that Jesus was so filled with love for us that He willingly bore the burden of our sins on the cross, God wants us to be so filled with love that we are willing to help bear the burden of others. We are in fact asked to be our brother's/sister's keeper.

We need only recall the story of Mary and Martha from Luke 10:38-42:

> *As they continued their journey he entered a village where a woman whose name was Martha welcomed him. She had a sister named Mary [who] sat beside the Lord at his feet listening to him speak. Martha, burdened with much serving, came to him and said, "Lord, do you not care that my sister has left me by myself to do the serving? Tell her to help me." The Lord said to her in reply, "Martha, Martha, you are anxious and worried about many things. There is need of only one thing. Mary has chosen the better part and it will not be taken from her."*

There is more to learn from the story of Jesus washing the feet of the disciples. From John 13:12-17:

> *So when he had washed their feet and put his garments back on and reclined at table again, he said to them, "Do you realize what I have done for you? You call me "teacher" and "master", and rightly so, for indeed I am. If I, therefore, the master and teacher, have washed your feet, you ought to wash one another's feet. I have given you a model*

to follow, so that as I have done for you, you should also do. Amen, Amen, I say to you, no slave is greater than his master, nor any messenger greater than the one who sent him. If you understand this, blessed are you if you do it.

I do not always respond to the call to serve others with a loving heart. Far too often, I have feelings of frustration and impatience, of being overwhelmed, of being taken advantage of, of agreeing to do, but grumbling while doing. Yet in quiet, contemplative moments I realize that compared to what Jesus has done for me, anything I might do to help someone else is insignificant, at best. Clearly I need to be far more aware of how He serves me, because in doing so I will be more open to lovingly serve others.

One of our about-to-be modern-day saints, Blessed Mother Teresa of Calcutta, recast Jesus' instruction into different words. One of her most famous quotes is: "We cannot do great things. We can only do little things with great love." What a remarkable statement of humility.

I was reminded of this very sentiment during each of the three mission trips I have made to Honduras. Seemed to me that after all the fund raising, preparation, and travel to Comayagua, etc., what I wanted to do was work, work, work – to the point that knocking off on time at the end of the day was a significant irritation. If I am here to help, let me help. But dedicating my time exclusively to swinging a hammer would have significantly reduced the most deeply, spiritually moving parts of those trips – private and group prayer time, adoration, and personal reflection. In the end, we accomplished what we went for. And so much more!

Thank you, Jesus, for giving me your heart of service so that I can bring light to even more people! Help me never stray from your example.

Battling Our Goliaths

*The Lord of hosts has this to say: "It was I who took
you from the pasture and from the care of the flock to
be commander of my people Israel. I have been with
you wherever you were, and have destroyed all your
enemies before you. And I will make you famous like
the great ones of the earth." (2 Samuel 7:8-9)*

The story of David is fascinating – and one from which we
can all learn much. The epoch story of his life is chronicled
in the two books of Samuel. The historic accounts of David's
battle with Goliath while he was still quite young, his service
to King Saul, the perils of his eventual rise to king, his
sinfulness – all make for exciting reading. From the Psalms,
about half of which were written by David, we learn about
his personal journey by way of beautiful songs of emotion.
Some scholars maintain every emotion known to humans
is portrayed there. With David's up-and-down life journey,
he clearly experienced the full spectrum of emotions, from
unbridled love and joy to profound despair and lament.

There are many important life lessons we can learn from
David doing battle with Goliath, a story about both religion
and politics. How many times, however, have you heard to
never talk about either topic? I would add two more – never
talk about the politics of religion or the religion of politics.
Avoiding these subjects has almost become a mantra in
many families, in most organizations, and is characteristic

of sometimes fragile friendships. Have you ever wondered why? Is it because religion and politics are both emotionally heavily charged topics? Is it because we don't want to show our lack of knowledge or understanding? Is it because we do not have the courage to speak our mind and heart? Are we fearful of letting others know how we really feel? Or is it more likely a combination of all these reasons and maybe still others?

Back to David, Goliath and the Philistines. Imagine you are David and you have been sent by your father, Jesse, to take bread and cheese to your brothers and their comrade soldiers in Saul's army, encamped across the valley from the Philistine army. The soldiers have been there now for forty days. Keep in mind, by this time, Samuel had already anointed David as the one the Lord had chosen to lead His people, and David also was periodically asked to play the harp for Saul when Saul was down in the dumps. My point is, David would come and go between his father's flock and the army on a reasonably regular basis. For forty days, Goliath had been sneering at and insulting Saul's army, attempting to shame Saul into sending a soldier to fight him. At six-foot-six, no one had any interest in going one-on-one with Goliath. So there both army's sat – mostly looking at each other – for nearly six weeks, both too proud to walk away, neither being willing to take the offensive, although Goliath was working hard to instigate a fight he knew he would win, and in winning the Philistines would enslave Saul's army. By this time, Saul had abdicated any pretense of being a leader.

David delivered the food to his brothers and their buddies at the front line and while there witnessed Goliath going through his now daily hubris of insulting the Israelite army. In spite of the food he brought, David's brothers were less than thrilled to see him, and basically accused him of being irresponsible for leaving the sheep and for grandstanding by showing up at the battlefield, mostly for the adrenalin rush. David, likely too young to fully understand why they resented him, was hurt by the way his brothers spoke to him. So he did what he often did, he went to talk with Saul. David was a pretty perceptive young man and realized that Saul was disheartened, confused, and discouraged at the situation.

David must have had a flood of emotions running through his heart. He likely was infuriated. Here was the army of Israel, being mocked and insulted by a Philistine. No doubt Goliath was a formidable opponent. But why were his brothers and the rest of Saul's army intimidated to the point of silence and inaction? Had they forgotten that they were God's chosen people? He likely was also embarrassed. And his king – surely he must have had some pangs of disappointment in Saul's lack of initiative.

So David went to Saul and volunteered to fight Goliath. Just imagine what that scene might have looked like. Saul finally accepted David's offer and decided that David should be clothed in his kingly armor, which clearly did not fit. David eventually headed out for the fight without armor, equipped with five rocks in his pocket, plus a leather slingshot. The rest is history. Good overcame evil, small overcame mighty, and courage overcame paralyzing fear.

What can we learn from these events? What lessons play into our daily lives? What Goliaths are out there that we fear, and because we are fearful we shy away from and/or remain silent? I will offer just a few.

Not long ago, the United States Supreme Court upheld an Oregon law that legitimizes some forms of assisted suicide. How is it in our society we have come to believe that as God's children we have the right to meddle in His plans for us? Do we really believe we have the right to be in control of when we die? Many do, but many of us who do not are unwilling to voice our beliefs.

Several years ago, the movie "Brokeback Mountain" won the Golden Globe award for best movie of the year, and although it did not win an Oscar for best motion picture, it did win Academy Awards in three other categories. The movie storyline is about two gay cowboys. Following the awards ceremonies, a commentator on EWTN (Eternal Word Television Network) radio said that the movie was still another not so subtle attempt by the very liberal minded movie industry to numb our senses to homosexuality and thereby begin to reduce our inclination to be shocked, and as our shock lessens then to accept it as normal. Isn't it odd that such a movie would win best movie, but the beautifully powerful and moving *Passion of the Christ* did not?

In 2006, members of the Senate Judiciary Committee grilled Samuel Alito for three days attempting to trip him up so he would disclose whether he would help overturn Roe v. Wade should the issue come before him as an Associate Justice. The underlying tone of the probing questioning implied that anyone who holds pro life beliefs is certainly not worthy to sit on the highest court in the land.

For the past several Christmas seasons, numerous retail companies decided that Christmas was a four-letter word for their employees and that 'holiday' greetings would replace Merry Christmas. Still other retailers banned Salvation Army bell-ringers from collecting donations. An interesting side-bar story in this issue is that a Jewish activist group picketed on the streets of New York in favor of the Christian position of Christmas (in part because Christians were not making enough noise themselves, and because it has been through the support of Christians in the United States that Jewish people have always been able to celebrate Hanukkah!) Why are so many of us unwilling to protest verbally or if not verbally, at least financially, when our freedoms of speech and religion are challenged?

How is it in a country where about eighty-five percent of the population claims to be Christian, we seem to be so afraid to express our beliefs? Granted, far fewer than one hundred percent of those declaring they are Christian actively practice their religion, but our Christian tradition, which is tolerant of others beliefs, does not require that we remain silent in the face of Goliath-sized insults. Yet many of us do remain so because of fear, indifference, embarrassment, etc.

On a much smaller, personal scale, how about making the sign of the cross and saying a mealtime blessing while dining out? I used to avoid making the sign of the cross in public, choosing instead to make a small cross on my chest and mumbling the words so no one would see or hear (that is, if I remembered to pray at all). An even greater challenge is to lead a mealtime blessing (or at least pausing to say one silently) while dining with a business associate.

How about standing up in support of a colleague or friend at work or in a social setting when someone is talking negatively about them behind their back? On the flip side, how about refusing to speak ill of anyone when they are absent?

How about insisting on doing the right thing in your workplace, even when doing so is unpopular? Shave a little here, a little there, who will know? Or often, justifying our behavior by telling yourself what I'm doing is tiny in comparison to the resources of this mega-corporation.

Christians should protest loudly the airing of TV shows like the 'Book of Daniel' that treated Jesus in a painfully cavalier way. Maybe we should protest financially by refusing to support sponsors of such shows – or protest vocally to the local TV stations that air them. As it turned out, NBC's plan to air thirteen episodes of that particular series was dropped after only four, primarily because of the network's inability to get sponsors. The public's outrage in this case was heard loud and clear.

As April 15 approaches each year, would it really matter in the big scheme of things if I "adjusted" my charitable contributions in my favor or "conveniently forgot" to report all of my income?

I guess there really are reasons why so many people avoid talking about the religion of politics and the politics of religion.

As we read the account of David and Goliath, as we visualize the events that took place on the battle field in the Valley of Terebinth, and likely think it strange that two armies basically sat and looked at each other for more than a month, it might be easy to ridicule the silence and inaction by Saul's army in the face of insults by Goliath the Philistine. But we face similar challenges nearly every day. Our society throws many Goliaths in our path. The question then becomes: Do we (I) have the courage of David to face those challenges and act decisively? David went into battle with a slingshot and a handful of smooth rocks. But he also carried with him the power of the Holy Spirit – the very same Holy Spirit that is the source of our strength to go against giants of all sorts.

Are you (am I) open to accepting the strength that comes from allowing the Holy Spirit to work in your (my) life?

Reflection

XIV

We Seem to Live in a World of Opposites

And many false prophets will arise and lead many astray. (Matthew 25:11)

In the summer of 2012, my wife and I had the opportunity to attend a theatrical presentation of C. S. Lewis's, *The Screwtape Letters*. Lewis is considered by many to be one of the finest intellects of the twentieth century, and *The Screwtape Letters* one of his best works. Among his other well-known works are, *Mere Christianity*, the *Tales of Narnia* series, *The Great Divorce*, *The Four Loves*, and many more. All of his works are deeply spiritual, including the Narnia tales, but interestingly, while Lewis is acclaimed most for his magnificent, spiritually rich writing, he was a reformed atheist!! Fortunately, he came to see the folly of those empty beliefs and turned himself in a positive direction – and how.

For those who may be unfamiliar with *The Screwtape Letters*, the easiest way to summarize the book is that it is a series of letters written by Screwtape, a master devil, who is mentoring his devil-in-training nephew, Wormwood, on how to lead patients (or clients) down the path to eternal destruction. In his instructions to Wormwood, Screwtape actually teaches deeply spiritual concepts, but does so from the dark side – that is, from the devil's point of view. The book is considered by many literary critics as likely the finest example of reverse psychology ever written, particularly in a spiritual sense.

In the theatrical presentation we attended, Screwtape is the only person with a speaking part; however, there is another actor on stage who says nothing, except for periodically making some troubled, guttural noises, while flailing about in possessed ways. The nonverbal actor is Screwtape's devil secretary who takes dictation. During the one hour and fifty-minute performance, without an intermission, Screwtape delivers roughly twenty-five percent of the entire text of the book, one marvelous letter after another. The monologue is simply brilliant (and the presentation extraordinary). In many of the letters, Screwtape urges Wormwood to tempt his patient into getting involved in a variety of activities, including church-related ministries, doing what could be noble but doing so for his own reward versus doing it because of a desire to truly and selflessly serve others. My favorite letter is the one in which Screwtape, writes:

> Dear Wormwood, I see only one thing to do at the moment. Your patient has become humble; have you drawn his attention to the fact? All virtues are less formidable to us once the man is aware that he has them, but this is especially true of humility. Catch him at the moment when he is really poor in spirit and smuggle into his mind the gratifying reflection, "By Jove! I'm being humble," and almost immediately pride – pride at his own humility – will appear. If he awakes to the danger and tries to smother this new form of pride, make him proud of his attempt.

Screwtape further advises Wormwood:

> The great thing is to make him (the patient) value an opinion for some quality other than truth, thus introducing an element of dishonesty and make-believe into the heart of what otherwise threatens to become a virtue. By this method thousands of

humans have been brought to think that humility means pretty women trying to believe they are ugly and clever men trying to believe they are fools. The Enemy (God) wants to bring the man to a state of mind (in) which he could design the best cathedral in the world, and know it to be the best, and rejoice in the fact, without being any more (or less) or otherwise glad at having done it than he would be if it had been done by another.

What remarkable genius to teach morality and spirituality using the voice and tricks of Satan himself. Remarkable, too, how obvious the *right* path becomes when we are intellectually (and knowingly) led down the path of evil. Funny how we see the actions of others modeling the evil ways Screwtape teaches, yet how oblivious we seem to be to our own shortcomings. The first time I read *The Screwtape Letters* that was my experience. During the second reading, however, the veil was removed from my eyes, and I saw the reality of how so much of my own behavior seemed to be following the opposite path than the one I should be on. The warning Jesus gave us about removing the log from our own eye before removing the splinter from our brother's eye, came flooding into my consciousness. I could go on with similar examples of Lewis' genius, but will leave it to you to read from his work on your own.

Opposites even show up in our prayer life. How often do we pray to our loving Father, and conclude He must be asleep (as we know dads fall asleep easily) because we are not getting immediate answers to what surely are our most important needs? But being asleep and answering our prayers in His time rather than our time are quite different. God answers in His time – for our good – not in our time.

We can learn much from seeing and experiencing opposites, but clearly not all of what we learn is positive.

Cursory analysis of current events yields proof that living with opposites, contradictions, and saying one thing while meaning another are realities. Hold on to that thought for a minute.

After lunch July 4, 2012, the ten adult family members who were gathered around our table shared the responsibility of reading aloud the Declaration of Independence. For me, like most of our guests, hearing the words of one of the most important documents in our nation's history was quite sobering, particularly because it had been quite a long time since any of us had read it. At the time the Declaration was written, the political philosophy it represented was not new; its ideals of individual liberty had already been expressed some years before by John Locke and the Continental philosophers. What Jefferson did, however, was to summarize this philosophy as "self-evident truths" and set forth a list of grievances against the King in order to justify before the world the breaking of ties between the colonies and the mother country. Even though those words were written about 240 years ago in a time that might seem very different than the present, they caused a stirring in all of us.

As we listened to Jefferson's words, detailing the reasons for the need to declare our independence from the tyrannies of the British crown, we all seemed to feel that history, in an odd sort of way, might be repeating itself. The conversation that followed highlighted how, in our current political environment, we are seeing challenges to many of the rights that we frankly have taken for granted for more than two centuries. For example, we have recently seen:

- Numerous instances where freedom of speech has been given priority over freedom of religion;
- Supreme Court decisions that establish policies that violate God's natural laws concerning marriage;

- Obstruction to civil debate on a wide range of exceptionally important issues such as health care and immigration, as demonstrated in the passage of the Affordable Care Act;
- Strong moves toward governance by way of Executive Orders that seeks to bypass our revered legislative process, that while messy, at least allows for dialogue on critical issues.

So now we find ourselves living in a nation that separated itself from a manipulative and arrogant despot 240 years ago so that we could be free, being manipulated by people we elected to continue and fully support those freedoms. Some of our elected officials, unfortunately, have chosen instead a path that challenges a great deal of what makes our republic, one nation, under God, indivisible, with liberty and justice for all. Many historians and political scientists believe in the 5000-year history of mankind there has never been a document that provided such clear guidance for a republic than the U.S. Constitution. Yet here we stand, many in our country stating forthrightly that the Constitution is simply outdated and no longer relevant. Talk about living in a world of opposites.

Isn't it hard to believe that implementing the Affordable Care Act provisions essentially mandates all employers to provide insurance that pays for birth control, sterilization and abortive procedures or be heavily fined (or is that taxed, no it must be fined, but the Supreme Court says taxed!!), regardless of the religious beliefs of the employer, or employee? Yet these same measures that claim to protect women's rights actually support multiple lines of life destructive processes. Rather than calling these mandates what they really are, much of the media has been co-opted into believing and supporting the notion that the Catholic Church and others are objecting to the Affordable Care Act regulations simply because the Church is against birth control. And while the Church does oppose artificial means of birth control, I find it both interesting and puzzling that a fundamental religious freedom issue has been rather effectively spun to be a birth control/abortion issue. Interesting, too, our Constitution says nothing about the right to use birth control, but it is very clear about religious freedom. The First Amendment is quite direct: "Congress shall make no law respecting an establishment of religion, or prohibiting the free exercise thereof." However, if we are told that the ACA regulations requiring everyone's health insurance pay for artificial birth control, sterilization and abortive procedures are about women's rights (and the exact opposite is true) enough times, then to our society the regulations *become* about women's reproductive rights and not about religious freedom. Actually, at the religious rally preceding the Fortnight for Freedom held at Marist school in Atlanta in July 2012, Dr. Alveda King (Dr. Martin Luther King's niece and a non-Catholic) in her closing remarks, with her tongue imbedded deeply into her cheek, said the mandates were about women's rights – the right to higher incidences of heart disease and several forms of cancer, the right to take the life of an unborn baby, and the right to be promiscuous without repercussions. Fortunately, as the result of all this debate, numerous Catholic entities have followed the lead of Belmont Abbey College, and have sued the government over the interference with free exercise of our religious freedom. Bill Thierfelder, president of Belmont, was the pioneer in taking legal action; but others, both Catholic and non-Catholic, have joined the fight. God bless them for their courage.

Over the past several years a significant amount of the rhetoric that comes from our Nation's capital and elsewhere seems to focus on the premise that if we say something enough times, and get enough media coverage, even the blackest of lies will eventually be believed and adopted as truth. And while I am certainly no historian, I have studied enough to be aware that the methods used in Germany in the late 1920s and 1930s are eerily similar to what is going on in our "land-of-the-free" today. Say stuff enough times and regardless, people believe it, thus lies become truths and opposites become equals!

From 2 Chronicles 7:14 we are told:

If my people, which are called by my name, shall humble themselves, and pray, seek my face, and turn from their wicked ways; then will I hear from heaven, and will forgive their sin, and will heal their land.

Could there be a clearer message? In the midst of all the attacks on our religious freedom, humility and prayer are God's instructions for us. Throughout the Old Testament, we see, time and time again, how God's chosen people snubbed their noses at their heritage, went down their own arrogant paths, only to crash themselves against the fate they had been warned against. And those of us who should have learned from those hard-learned lessons of history, who surely would not find ourselves in a similar situation, in fact, find ourselves in a similar boat. Our pride, dependence on our own abilities, our arrogance both as individuals, as a Church and as a Nation, continues to plague us.

From 2 Corinthians, Chapter 12 we are told:

Brothers and sisters: That I, Paul, might not become too elated, because of the abundance of the revelations, a thorn in the flesh was given to me, an angel of Satan, to beat me, to keep me from being too elated. Three times I begged the Lord about this, which it might leave me, but he said to me, "My grace is sufficient for you, for power is made perfect in weakness." I will rather boast most gladly of my weaknesses, in order that the power of Christ

*may dwell with me. Therefore, I am content with
weaknesses, insults, hardships, persecutions, and
constraints, for the sake of Christ; for when I am
weak, then I am strong.*

If there ever was a time in our country's history to humble
ourselves, fall to our knees and turn to God in prayer, it is
now. Now is the time for us to align ourselves with one of the
more important tenants of Alcoholics' Anonymous, "Don't
worry about the future, rather be dedicated to doing the next
right thing." The next right thing in this moment is to pray,
pray, pray. I find *A Prayer for Religious Liberty*, frankly, to
be compelling:

Almighty God, Father of all nations, for freedom you
have set us free in Christ Jesus. We praise and bless
you for the gift of religious liberty, the foundation of
human rights, justice, and the common good. Grant
to our leaders the wisdom to protect and promote our
liberties; by your grace may we have the courage
to defend them, for ourselves and for all those who
live in this blessed land. We ask this through the
intercession of Mary Immaculate, our patroness, and
in the name of your Son, our Lord Jesus Christ, in
the unity of the Holy Spirit, with whom you live and
reign, one God, for ever and ever. Amen

There are absolute truths, given to us by our Creator, and
no frequency of denial will change them. Black is black.
White is white. No matter how many times I might say
black is white – it is not, and never will be. Similarly, our
religious freedom is an inalienable right not conferred on
us by our government, rather by our loving God. Allowing
others to relegate our religious freedom to second-class
status is simply wrong. We must courageously defend that

absolute right because it has been and must continue to be the foundation of our success as a republic.

Reflection

Filling the God-Shaped Vacuum –
Learning from Those in Need

*This is indeed the will of my Father, that all who see
the Son and believe in him may have eternal life; and
I will raise them up on the last day. (John 6:40)*

I have long believed that we create a fertile climate for
personal growth and learning (spiritual and otherwise) when
we allow ourselves to be open and aware of everything
around us. We can often be surprised by how and from
whom we learn.

Some time ago I read a profound quote attributed to the
famous seventeenth century mathematician, Blaise Pascal.
Pascal was born in France in 1623, the third of his parents
four children, but their only son. He was quite precocious.
In fact, in spite of his father's insistence that he not study
mathematics until he was fifteen, on his own, Blaise proved
that the sum of the angles of any triangle was 180 degrees –
two right angles. His father relented. By the age of seventeen,
Pascal had already published papers on the development of
some of the most important building blocks in the foundation
of projective geometry, particularly those dealing with conic
sections. His reputation among the leading mathematicians
of his time grew quickly.

Young Pascal built the first digital calculator to assist
his father who was a tax collector. Later he developed the
underlying concepts for probability theory. His work on

binomial coefficients played a pivotal role in Isaac Newton's discovery of the general binomial theorem for fractional and negative powers. And his work in the field of physics, particularly his *Treatise on the Equilibrium of Liquids* (1653), in which he explains Pascal's law of pressure, is a complete outline of a system of hydrostatics, the first in the history of science.

With all of these mathematical and scientific credentials, Pascal does not really sound like the kind of guy you might expect to be a source of profound philosophical and theological insight, but he was!

So, let me explain as clearly as I am able, the connection between Pascal and my first experience as a missionary to Honduras. As it happens, Blaise Pascal was a devout Catholic when he was young, faltered after the death of his father, but renewed the devout practice of his faith after a near death experience at the age of 32. During some of the most productive years of his research into complex mathematical and physical processes, he published several notable works in philosophy and theology, the most famous of which was entitled, *Pensées*, which is a collection of personal thoughts on human suffering and faith in God. This work contains *Pascal's Wager* which claims to prove that belief in God is rational with the following argument:

> If God does not exist, one will lose nothing by believing in Him, while if He does exist, one will lose everything by not believing.

While he used probabilistic and mathematical arguments, his main conclusion was:

> ...we are compelled to gamble...Belief is a wise wager. Granted that faith cannot be proved, what harm will come to you if you gamble on its truth and it proves false? If you gain, you gain all; if you lose,

you lose nothing. Wager, then, without hesitation, that He exists.

Pascal's Wager has caused many in doubt to realize they have nothing to lose and everything to gain by putting their faith in God. Enough background.

The thought by Pascal mentioned at the outset of this reflection and the one I want to use as a central theme here, is one I find quite compelling:

> There is a God shaped vacuum in the heart of every man which cannot be filled by any created thing, but only by God, the Creator, made known through Jesus.

I would ask that you hold that thought. "A God-shaped hole in the heart of every man..."

Several years ago, nearly two dozen missionaries from our parish embarked on a trip to Honduras (my first) to serve not only as representatives of our parish but also minister to the poor in Comayagua. We were met at the airport in Tegucigalpa by Father Herald and Brother Mateo, members of the Franciscan Friars of the Renewal (CFR's), then made the 60-mile drive to Comayagua and Casa Guadeloupe, our home for the next twelve days.

Casa Guadeloupe (at the time of our visit there) was a facility that had as its centerpiece a beautiful open air chapel, accommodations for 250 visitors, meeting/class rooms, kitchen and dining rooms and facilities for local residents to shower and wash clothes. Many of the neighbors are so poor they do not even have running water, so the friars make safe, potable water available for them to take home. Much of the area in the barrio around Casa G resembles the pictures we saw of Baghdad during the height of the Iraqi war – trash and rubble everywhere. Standing water is also a real issue, especially during the rainy season. One day, driving past an intermittent pond Brother Nathaniel referred to it as 'malaria pond', and the next day, 'Dengue pond'. Not surprising, local children would be swimming in the pond each day, even though the risk of disease from the water was high.

Our first weekend was spent serving food and cleaning up for a large retreat of nearly three hundred young people between the ages of fifteen and twenty-five. The retreat was conducted in the format of Youth 2000, and frankly, even without any understanding of Spanish, the experience for most of us was quite profound. I found myself studying the faces of the attendees and their faces spoke volumes. Music throughout our stay was provided by three of the Brothers who were each excellent guitarists and vocalists, and a visiting Sister (a concert-quality cellist). Several other local musicians and vocalists joined the CFR's for the retreat.

Probably the highlight of the youth retreat for me was on Saturday evening with an event called the Eucharistic Procession. I have been a Catholic my entire life, but never experienced such a profound event. For most of the retreat, the Blessed Sacrament was openly exposed, sitting atop a five-foot-high, four-sided wooden structure, with six tiers of three candles per tier on each of the four sides. Following a rather lengthy spiritual build up (in Spanish, of course), the Brothers began moving the participants into a series of concentric circles around the Blessed Sacrament. Then, Father John Anthony took the Blessed Sacrament and began moving past each person, stopping for 10-15 seconds for personal adoration by each person, touching the base of the monstrance to their head. From the very beginning, I knew the experience would be profound.

Watching the faces of the young people as the Blessed Sacrament approached them was amazing – and while I could describe many, I will tell you about one, a young man I had watched the evening before. Long before Father John approached him with the Blessed Sacrament, he had dropped to his knees, bowed low, and with his face nearly to the floor he began to sob. For the nearly fifteen minutes he awaited the presence of Jesus next to him, he quietly, but deeply sobbed. When Father John approached him, the boy did not rise – so Father John knelt down to him. I must confess I was deeply moved by the sight before me. And it was in that very moment I recalled the quote by Blaise Pascal – "There is a God shaped vacuum in the heart of every man which cannot be filled by any created thing, but only by God, the Creator, made known through Jesus." While some of us try to fill that vacuum with success, with our work, with money, with alcohol, drugs, stuff, whatever, I believe I saw, at that moment the vacuum in that young man's heart filled to the brim with Jesus Christ. Part of the God shaped vacuum in my heart was filled as well.

On Monday, we began two separate work activities. Half of our group conducted a vacation bible school for about 300 children from the nearby barrio and Catholic orphanages for which the CFR's provide spiritual support – one for girls, the other for boys. The other half of us began tackling three specific projects at a boys' orphanage called *El Granja (Hogar de ninos, Jesus de Nazaretho)*. *Granja* is a Catholic home to 81 boys. We were asked to build a large (14 x 32 foot) sun shelter next to a concrete pad or arena where the boys play soccer and where the CFR's celebrate outdoor masses for the boys. The second task was to strip and paint the beds for every one of the boys. The third and final task was to lay out, dig and pour the concrete footer for a pig pen to house 6 pigs. As we started, we really thought the pig pen project would not even get started (could be that was wishful thinking), but as the week progressed we realized it would. As it happened, the boys had a week off from school, so many of the older boys and even some of the younger ones worked alongside of us on all three projects.

The shelter we built had concrete support posts with steel beams welded to reinforcing rods extending from the top of the concrete, cross member steel beams, and galvanized steel roofing attached to the cross members. The beds were sanded and painted by members of our missionary crew with a lot of help from the boys. They looked great when finished. They had some paint sprayer problems the first day, so getting started was a bit shaky, but after adjustments significant progress was made. Both the beds and shelter were completed by the time we returned to Casa Guadalupe on Thursday afternoon. On Wednesday, with some shifts in the size of the crews, several of us began work on the pig pen – an effort that was physically challenging because of the rocky soil. On Friday, all of the construction crew, except for three who were commandeered to repair the roof of a poor woman our missionaries had helped the previous year, worked on the pig pen.

I cannot say enough positive things about the boys with whom we worked. Many already had trade skills that were useful including welding, cutting steel, mixing, pouring and finishing concrete, spray painting, etc. Education for most of the boys involves a half day of conventional school and a half day learning job skills at Granja. The boys worked hard, had initiative, were polite, had good senses of humor and put up with our inabilities, particularly with their language. Had it not been for their participation we would simply not have been able to accomplish all we did. Our entire missionary team went back to Granja on Saturday morning where we were presented souvenirs made by the boys, and given an opportunity for them and for us to express our gratitude for the week.

I had a really hard time saying goodbye to the half-dozen or so young men that I worked so closely with during the week – Francisco, Dennis, Daniel, Roberto, Christian, and Ramon. Seeing the deep faith and devotion these (and other) young men at Granja have, along with the hope for their future clearly visible in their eyes, certainly helped fill some more of the God-shaped vacuum in my heart.

The missionaries involved with the vacation bible school experienced many of the same feelings as those of us on the construction crew. While I was not at Casa Guadalupe for their programs, we did come back early one day because of storms, to hear the sound of more than a hundred small children singing hymns, led by the Brothers. Their blended voices sounded like a choir of angels singing – it was simply beautiful. Hearing them filled a little more of the God shaped vacuum in my heart.

A few final thoughts...The Friars are a special group of men, renaissance men. They are musicians, engineers, vocalists, nurses, former military officers – but first and foremost men of God who have given up almost everything earthly, to serve the poorest of the poor. The sisters are, also, an equally amazing group – in addition to the concert cellist, another was a world class speed skater who finished sixth in the 1998 Winter Olympics.

Early in the week I went to confession to Father Herald. For my penance, he asked that I carefully observe and decide (by the end of the week) who was the most humble person I encountered while in Comayagua. Not sure I have ever had such a difficult penance. Praying three Our Fathers and three Hail Marys would have been much easier. Every member of the religious community was a contender. But many of the people we were blessed to serve were, too. Most of them, who have nearly nothing, maintain a deep and abiding faith in God and hope that He will somehow provide. In their poverty, they remain rich. Matthew Kelly's words from his book, *The Art of Loving and the Joy of Being Loved*, seem to ring particularly loud, "We can never get enough of what we don't really need." The friars and the poor were living examples of the reality that we do not really need much to be happy if we are faithful.

Having had the opportunity to provide a very small amount of assistance to a few in Honduras was a remarkable experience, one that allowed me to develop a far deeper and more profound understanding of what it means to minister to other members of the Body of Christ. The God-shaped hole in my heart has been made smaller by this experience. In his final homily at Mass just before we left to return to Atlanta, Father Herald told us a story that Brother Damien (an experienced ER nurse) tells. Brother Damian said he could always tell whether a doctor in the ER had ever gone on a medical mission simply by the way they treated their patients upon their return. Father Herald then asked – what now, when you return? Will others be able to notice any difference in you?

I can only hope and pray my wife, my family, friends, fellow parishioners, others at large, are able (and continue to be able) to observe my behavior and know that I have been so positively impacted by this experience. Surely the part of the God-shaped vacuum in my heart filled in Honduras should be evident in my behavior.

I offer a special prayer of thanksgiving for the people of Honduras and the generous gift they were to me during all three of my visits there.

Our Lady of Guadalupe, pray for us.

Reflection

XVI

The Seeming Paradox of Nondualistic Thinking as Seen in the Story of the Prodigal Son from the Servant's Perspective

While he was still a long way off, his father caught sight of him, and was filled with compassion. He ran to his son, embraced him and kissed him.
(Luke 15:20)

The thoughts and feelings in this reflection came to me in the quiet solitude of a silent retreat my wife and I attended a while back at Ignatius House, a Jesuit retreat facility in Atlanta. As obtuse as the title of this reflection may sound at this moment, I hope to connect all the dots by the end of it.

One of the early sessions at the retreat focused on Luke 15:11-32, the story of the Prodigal Son. We were asked to follow carefully the narrative as it was read, in a way that might be different than how we might have read or listened to it before. The retreat master asked us to select a character in the story, and then listen to the story from inside the head, heart, and clothes of that person. It did not matter which character we chose, we were to just pick one and stay with that person throughout. I would ask you to do the same now as you read the passage. If you have done this before, choose a different character than the one you were before. The narrative of the story follows:

Jesus continued: "There was a man who had two sons. The younger one said to his father, 'Father, give me my share of the estate.' So he divided his property between them. Not long after that, the younger son

135

got together all he had, set off for a distant country and there squandered his wealth in wild living. After he had spent everything, there was a severe famine in that whole country, and he began to be in need. So he went and hired himself out to a citizen of that country, who sent him to his fields to feed pigs. He longed to fill his stomach with the pods that the pigs were eating, but no one gave him anything. When he came to his senses, he said, 'How many of my father's hired men have food to spare, and here I am starving to death! I will set out and go back to my father and say to him: 'Father, I have sinned against heaven and against you. I am no longer worthy to be called your son; make me like one of your hired men.' So he got up and went to his father. But while he was still a long way off, his father saw him and was filled with compassion for him; he ran to his son, threw his arms around him and kissed him. The son said to him, 'Father, I have sinned against heaven and against you. I am no longer worthy to be called your son.' But the father said to his servants, 'Quick! Bring the best robe and put it on him. Put a ring on his finger and sandals on his feet. Bring the fattened calf and kill it. Let's have a feast and celebrate. For this son of mine was dead and is alive again; he was lost and is found.' So they began to celebrate.

Meanwhile, the older son was in the field. When he came near the house, he heard music and dancing. So he called one of the servants and asked him what was going on. 'Your brother has come,' he replied, 'and your father has killed the fattened calf because he has him back safe and sound.'

The older brother became angry and refused to go in. So his father went out and pleaded with him. But he answered his father, 'Look! All these years I've been slaving for you and never disobeyed your orders. Yet you never gave me even a young goat so I could celebrate with my friends. But when this son of yours who has squandered your property with prostitutes comes home, you kill the fattened calf for him!' 'My son,' the father said, 'you are always with me, and everything I have is yours. But now we must celebrate and rejoice, because your brother was dead and has come to life again; he was lost and has been found.'"

So which person in the story did you follow? The Prodigal Son? How about the Father? Did you put yourself in the position of being the "Loyal Son"? I have actually gone through this exercise multiple times in the past, and have put myself in the place of each of these three main characters. But for some reason, when the retreat director challenged us with this exercise, I did something I had never done before — I put myself into the role of a minor character. There were other characters you know!

As I listened to the story, I found myself in the role of the servant. Servants in the time of Jesus tended to be quite loyal to their masters, and no doubt that is true in this story. The term servant does not show up in the story until half way through. The concept of servant appears first when the Prodigal Son was mentally (or maybe audibly) composing his song of self-pity. *"How many of my father's hired men have food to spare, and here I am starving to death! I will set out and go back to my father and say to him: Father, I have sinned against heaven and against you. I am no longer worthy to be called your son; make me like one of your hired men."* The son could just as easily have said "Father, make me one of your servants. I will work for you and be loyal to you, but I can clearly no longer be your son – I don't deserve that after what I have done."

At my master's side, I hear the father say *"Quick! Bring the best robe and put it on him. Put a ring on his finger and sandals on his feet. Bring the fattened calf and kill it. Let's have a feast and celebrate. For this son of mine was dead and is alive again; he was lost and is found."* I jump to the task, with a level of excitement I have not felt for a long time. I spend so much time serving my master (the father) I have really been down in a very low spot ever since the younger son decided to leave. My master was devastated. The look of hurt on his face was obvious to everyone, particularly me. With one sentence, the boy had driven a stake through his father's heart. In spite of his anguish, my master asked me to help his son pack for the journey, not knowing whether he would ever see him again. And now he's back – broken, embarrassed, humbled – but home. My master cannot contain his joy. He asks me to fetch the finest robe, sandals for his feet, and a grand ring (no doubt a gold ring) for his finger. In a brief moment, my master's grief has turned to unexplainable joy. His joy is now my joy.

But…there is actually another servant mentioned as well. *"Meanwhile, the older son was in the field. When he came near the house, he heard music and dancing. So he called one of the servants and asked him what was going on. 'Your brother has come,' he replied, 'and your father has killed the fattened calf because he has him back safe and sound."* As I thought about this passage, I sensed that I was a different servant, the one who worked side-by-side with the loyal son, and while we were clearly master and servant, we also have a close relationship. As his servant (and likely friend) I frankly struggled to give him the news of his brother. So many emotions had been shared, so much anger had been felt, so much resentment had built up. But I had to tell him the truth, even knowing that doing so would be difficult. And it was. His reaction was hardly a surprise.

Later that evening, the two servants were together in the servants' quarters and began talking about the events of the day. As the father's servant, I commented that I was simply thrilled at what had happened earlier in the day, the joy that erupted and the celebration that ensued. As the loyal son's servant, I related that my day had not gone nearly the same, because my master had the proverbial rug jerked out from under him. His worthless, philandering brother had returned, hat in hand, and the old man fell for his sob story, and accepted him back. What a terrible day.

As they talked, the two servants realized they were actually describing the same event, essentially telling the same story but from two very different perspectives. How could we be talking about the same thing, with two completely different outcomes? Can't you just see the looks on their faces and hear the tones of their voices? The conversation might have gone like this:

(Father's servant): "How could the Prodigal Son's return not be cause for celebration?"

(Loyal son's servant): "Are you kidding me!? How could the return of that good-for-nothing jerk possibly mean "party time"! He squandered everything he had, violated every rule the Jews hold sacred, embarrassed his father and caused him pain, not to mention what he did to my master, his older brother, who has hardly been recognized as his father's son."

I think it worthwhile to point out here that we see the world as we are, not as it is. Let me repeat, we see the world as we are, not as it is. Translated – our reality is formed from the place where we stand.

My feelings as the father's servant and my loyalty to him caused me to take on his unbridled joy. Imagine, his son, in some metaphorical way returned from the dead. How could I not be happy for my master?

As the loyal son's servant, I knew and even felt some of the same level of anger, hurt, and frustration, as the older son did. I had heard him speak so often of his feelings as we worked shoulder to shoulder in the fields. And now, after all the years of loyal service to his dad, he felt he was being kicked to the curb. What a fine "how do you do."

All of what I have just described went on in my mind and heart at the retreat, in an instant, far quicker than it took me to relay the story. But then I was shocked at where my thoughts and emotions took me next. What if the father's servant and the loyal son's servant were the SAME servant? Can you imagine the internal conflict? What a paradox, the father was joyful, and because of the same event, the loyal son was furious. Hold these thoughts for a moment.

Father Richard Rohr, a Franciscan priest, author, and director of the Center for Action and Contemplation, during most of his retreats and in his books, talks and writes about the fact that nearly all humans, particularly those of us in the Western world, use what he calls dualistic thinking. By way of very brief explanation, dualistic thinking is the way of thinking characterized by our seeing or judging things as either-or, right or wrong, good or bad, my way or the highway. In his book, *The Naked Now – Learning to see as the Mystics See*, Rohr suggests that to begin overcoming this type of thinking we must always start each encounter with a fundamental "yes" – in short if we do the opposite, we basically poison the well. To start with a "no" is largely what it means to be unconscious, unaware, polarized, dug-in. We eventually become so defensive that we cannot love or see well, and so defensive we cannot change. To be sure, there clearly are either-or situations, right or wrong situations, etc.; however, in some of the most important issues of our existence, dualistic thinking will simply prevent us from growing in understanding and tolerance.

In my first book, *Some Practical Lessons in Leadership – Observations from Daily Life*, I described the remarkable value of true dialogue, a form of conversation that takes place in the presence of an "abundance mentality." Dialogue is a particularly powerful catalyst for clarifying understanding. When just one person chooses not to see issues as good or bad, right or wrong, and not see debates as battles to be won or lost, we greatly increase our ability to develop deeper understanding. In their book, *Crucial Conversations*, Patterson, Grenny, McMillan, and Switzler refer to this mutual gathering of information as "filling the pool of shared meaning."

Rohr calls this "gathering" the beginning of nondual thinking. He states that nondual thinking is a way of seeing that refuses to eliminate the negativism, the problematic, the threatening parts of everything. It rejects any way that too quickly says, "That is not possible!" or "That does not make sense!" Instead, nondualistic thinking actually clarifies and sharpens our rational minds and increases our ability to see truthfully because our biases and fears are out of the way. Many of our most fundamental beliefs as Catholics mandate nondual thinking. Mary is Virgin and Mother. Jesus is human and divine. There is only one God, but three distinct persons. The Eucharist looks like bread but *IS* the body of Christ—the true presence.

Nondual thinking embraces the problematic, the seeming contradictions and the paradoxes, the very conflicting thoughts and feelings that the servant in the story of the Prodigal Son must have been thinking and feeling. He was joyful with the father's joy; he was sad because of the loyal son's pain; and sympathetic with the returning son's embarrassment and pathetic state upon his return. I preferred

141

to believe that the servant was able to embrace and live all three of those experiences at the same time.

We all have the capacity to internalize and understand such contradictions, and live comfortably with such paradoxes. But we cannot do so with polarized or dualistic thinking. We cannot do so if we are highly judgmental. And we cannot do so if we are unwilling to change. According to Rohr, what sets the Mystics apart from the rest of civilization (Mystics are deeply spiritual geniuses) is their ability to keep their minds and hearts open, guided by a profound presence and acceptance of the Holy Spirit. Nondualistic thinking is based on knowing what the rules of the road are, but having the wisdom and courage to know when to move past the rules. If that sounds strange, simply look at the earthly life of Jesus. On the Sabbath, Jesus told the paralytic to pick up his mat and walk – a violation of the law. He touched the leper, but did not isolate Himself as called for in the law. He did not demand that the apostles strictly observe all of the cleansing rites. He sensitively, but forthrightly, told Martha that her sister Mary had chosen the better way, even as Martha was there busying herself with preparing His food. Following the rules explicitly is dualistic thinking. Knowing the rules and when it makes sense to move beyond them requires nondualistic thinking. As another example, in the 13th century, when Christians demonized Muslims even more than we do today, St. Francis of Assisi told his Franciscan confreres that if they found a page of the Koran, they should kiss it and place it on the altar. St. Francis' Christian truth was not fear based. He was able to honor God and holiness anywhere it was found.

Each of us will find inner joy, deep peace and contentment only when we stop judging, ranking, and categorizing people and things and just see them. We can only do so when we allow ourselves to be fully and unreservedly guided by the Holy Spirit.

I believe the Servant in the story of the Prodigal Son surely must have been a nondualistic thinker, capable of living through and not being paralyzed by the paradox he experienced when the Prodigal Son returned home. Can we, can I, do the same, particularly when reaching out and serving others? Can I do the same as I pursue the mission God has planned for me?

Reflection

The Foundation of Humility is Love

Do nothing out of selfishness or out of vainglory;
rather, humbly regard others as more important than
yourselves. (Philippians 2:3)

Throughout this book, I have written about my growing awareness and understanding of the importance of humility, especially as it relates to responsibilities we have as Christians, as Catholics. In each of those earlier situations, I mentioned that my understanding of what it means to be humble was (and frankly still is) in its infancy. This reflection is simply my next tiny step toward a fuller understanding of what it means to be humble, and in so doing live up to what God expects of us. Not surprisingly, Jesus lived His life on earth demonstrating this virtue for us.

In Philippians, Chapter 2:1-11, Saint Paul teaches:

If there is any encouragement in Christ, any solace in love, any participation in the Spirit, any compassion and mercy, complete my joy by being of the same mind, with the same love, united in heart, thinking one thing. Do nothing out of selfishness or out of vainglory; rather, humbly regard others as more important than yourselves, each looking out not for his own interests, but [also] everyone for those of others.

*Have among yourselves the same attitude that is also
yours in Christ Jesus, Who, though he was in the form
of God, did not regard equality with God something
to be grasped. Rather, he emptied himself, taking the
form of a slave coming in human likeness; and found
human in appearance, he humbled himself, becoming
obedient to death, even death on a cross. Because of
this, God greatly exalted him and bestowed on him
the name that is above every name, that at the name
of Jesus every knee should bend, of those in heaven
and on earth and under the earth, and every tongue
confess that Jesus Christ is Lord, to the glory of God
the Father.*

What is the source of or foundation for the humility
demonstrated by Christ? Could it be anything other than
pure love – a love so strong that Jesus would die for me; a
love that seems so overwhelming that on occasion I might
even doubt it; a love I do not deserve but in spite of my
sinfulness He showers me with it each moment of every day
of my existence?

With the help of some commentary from Peter Kreeft's,
The God Who Loves You, and from Holy Scripture, I would
like to explore just what that Father-love looks like, feels like
and tastes like. Kreeft's observations are lovingly brilliant.
So if anything I say here strikes a resilient chord, or sounds
truly profound, the idea was likely from him.

Probably the most beautiful love letter ever written by
the hand of man, inspired of course by the Holy Spirit, is
found in 1 Corinthians 13:1-3:

*If I speak in human and angelic tongues but do not
have love, I am a resounding gong or a clashing
cymbal. And if I have the gift of prophecy and
comprehend all mysteries and all knowledge; if I*

*have all faith so as to move mountains but do not
have love, I am nothing. If I give away everything I
own, and if I hand my body over so that I may boast
but do not have love, I gain nothing.*

Why did Paul start his tender explanation of love to the people of Corinth by describing what *love is not*, articulating a series of admonitions about misusing or misunderstanding the gifts they had come to value – speaking in tongues, prophesying, faith to move mountains, even dying a martyr's death?

Going back to the twelfth chapter of 1 Corinthians will help us understand the context of Chapter 13. In Chapter 12, Paul was basically dealing with what had become a major issue in the Christian community in Corinth – a case of one-upmanship about who was given the greatest gifts. Paul told them the story about how the church is one body, and that each of us are the various, different parts. If all were eyes, how would we hear? If we were all arms, how would we walk? If all were ears, how would we smell? In the church, some are to preach, some are to prophesy, some are to speak in tongues, some to interpret tongues, etc. Each of us is to live out the various gifts as we have been given. Tongues are not more important than ears, feet, hands, or nose. We each play important, albeit different roles in God's church. St. Paul used Chapter 12 to set the stage for the far more important conversation with the Corinthians (and us) about love, the greatest gift given to us by God.

Rhetorically, Paul said that if you are a great speaker or speak in tongues but do not do so with love, you are a noisy trash can. If you are the most eloquent and intellectual speaker, but use those gifts for selfish motives, you might as well beat a drum. The gifts of human or angelic tongues have value only when they are used with love, the kind of love that is unselfish, others-centered, and unconditional. The same is true for giving everything we have, even our lives. The giving is of no value unless we do so with love. As an aside, I have always been puzzled by this last admonition – the one that says that if I allow myself to be martyred, and do so without love, it was useless. One only needs to recall the events of 9-11 to realize that it is pretty easy to die a martyr for a cause without love – just what the terrorists did. By sharp contrast, twelve Coptic Christians were martyred in North Africa in early 2015, simply because they were Christians and refused to deny Christ.

But Saint Paul was not referring only to using gifts of tongues, prophesy, and other gifts of the Holy Spirit, without love. In fact, this line of thought extends equally to doing acts of kindness without love; to giving of our wealth without love; to doing anything that might, on the outside, look like something admirable, wholesome, and God-like, but without love. Let me give you a simple, but real, example that could happen to any of us – in fact, it has happened to me – far more than once. If a family member is sick or infirmed and I know that I must take care of him or her, but I do so without a loving heart, in spite of the loving act, if done without love, I am not doing God's will. I am, in fact, a clanging cymbal.

After St. Paul clearly explained that love is far more than just what we do, even demonstrating the gifts of the Holy Spirit, he described fifteen attributes of what love really is and is not, 1 Corinthians 13:4-7:

> *Love is patient, love is kind. It is not jealous, [love] is not pompous, it is not inflated, it is not rude, it does not seek its own interests, it is not quick-tempered, it does not brood over injury, it does not rejoice over wrongdoing but rejoices with the truth. It bears all things, believes all things, hopes all things, endures all things."*

Let's start with "Love is patient." Real patience is not a feeling; it must be much deeper. Patience, driven by a selfless love, does not depend on feelings. How many of us have prayed for patience, but in truth we prayed, "Lord, give me patience, and do it now!"? Most people in our Western society have an inaccurate view of patience. One place I personally witnessed true patience was in Honduras. Each year, missionaries from our parish work with the Franciscan Friars of the Renewal in Comayagua. The Friars not only have the gift of patience they allow patience to guide virtually all their work. Very little of what they do is for immediate results, except providing emergency food and water. Instead, they take a much longer term approach to building the capacity of the poor to fend for themselves. Their help is temporary until those they minister to can take care of their own needs. Situations that develop over a very long time, seldom, if ever can be turned around in the short term. Real patience, underlain by an unconditional, others-centered love requires understanding and perseverance, not feelings that tend to be ephemeral. A reporter once tried to box Mother Teresa into a corner, asking over and over how she dealt with defeat (of poverty) every day in the streets of Calcutta. She finally replied, "God does not ask us to be successful, He asks us to be faithful." She could just as easily have answered that God does not ask us to feel good, He asks us to love, unconditionally. In self-examination, while trying to do kind things for others in need, I often fall short of doing so patiently or lovingly. While I might self-justify by saying to myself at least I tried, doing so is very much akin to saying that "I am proud of being humble." Tough (or should I say foolhardy) to attempt to rectify opposites being equal. For each of the fifteen characteristics of love in St. Paul's discourse, similar arguments can be made.

As Catholics, we have a wonderful heritage to study and emulate through the lives of the saints. One such giant is St.

John of the Cross, a contemporary of St. Teresa of Avila. He was a man known most for his teaching and devotion to the Cross. Serene, calm, and at peace in his own personal life even under harsh, cruel persecution by his confreres, John did not retaliate, did not deal brusquely, rudely or severely with others. He was gentle, meek, humble, benign and forgiving. Unwittingly he gave us a portrait of his own manner when he sketched out his counsel on how all of us are to behave under duress. "A soul enkindled with love is a gentle, meek, humble and patient soul...A soul that is hard because of its self-love grows harder." He further advised us to "Keep spiritually tranquil in a loving attentiveness to God, and when it is necessary to speak, let it be with the same calm and peace." People deeply in love with God invariably develop a habit of amiable and compassionate responses to those whom God Himself loves.

Saint John Vianney, the Cure' of Ars, patron saint of priests, is another example from our rich history demonstrating how exceptional love backed by exceptional actions impacts others. John was far from the brightest student in the seminary. In fact, he finished at the bottom of his class. After he was finally ordained, he was assigned to the small backwater town of Ars, France, population 230 people. The hamlet was located far from almost everything. He actually got lost on his initial trip there. He quickly discovered Mass attendance was poor and few entered the confessional. As time passed and his flock got to know him, they began filling the church and standing in line to go to confession. His reputation for loving, humble counsel grew and people began traveling long distances under difficult circumstances, often from other countries to be ministered to by him. His simple message of love and understanding touched the hearts of tens of thousands and he sometimes spent as much as eighteen hours a day hearing confessions. About prayer he said," Prayer is the inner bath of love into

150

which the soul plunges itself." His actions were guided by that bath of love.

The deeper we look, the more intensely we study and experience, the more we will surely grow in awareness that truly *God Is Love*. But, God is not a feeling. Loving feelings are actually the dribbles of love that we receive quite passively. Nothing about God is passive. God is warm, close to us, unconditional, fiery and dynamic. His love for us never fails, it never wavers, never stops.

In putting the bookend on his love letter, Paul concludes, 1 Corinthians 13:8-13:

> *Love never fails. If there are prophecies, they will be brought to nothing; if tongues, they will cease; if knowledge, it will be brought to nothing. For we know partially and we prophesy partially, but when the perfect comes, the partial will pass away. When I was a child, I used to talk as a child, think as a child, reason as a child; when I became a man, I put aside childish things. At present we see indistinctly, as in a mirror, but then face to face. At present I know partially; then I shall know fully, as I am fully known. So faith, hope, love remain, these three; but the greatest of these is love.*

When we look deeply at these final few verses we see a litany of many of the gifts that we hold dear in this life seemingly being brought to nothing (prophesies will be brought to nothing, tongues will cease, knowledge will go away). But what the finale says is that all we know in this life will pale by comparison to what we will know and experience in eternity. We will talk not like a child but as an adult. We will put childish thoughts away. We will see clearly, even more clearly than we see ourselves now in a mirror. We will no longer see partially; instead all knowledge and truth will

151

be ours. And while we will have all those things in heaven, we can begin or at least approach experiencing them in this life as well.

In our current human state, the three theological virtues that guide us are faith, hope and charity. As described in an earlier reflection entitled, "Love God, Love Your Neighbor," when we reach our eternal victory and stand before God in complete awe (i.e. experience the beatific vision), we will have no need for faith or hope. Most of our space exploration vehicles have a three stage propulsion system that moves them toward their destination, but the only part that actually goes into orbit is the essence of the rocket. In a similar way, when we reach our reward, we will jettison faith and hope because they are no longer needed. The third stage or state, whether we call it love, charity, or *agape*, is all we need. Hence, the greatest of these three is love.

How much does God love you? How much does He love me? How much does He love each and every one of us, individually? Let me answer by way of a visual image (I regret I do not know where I read this, thus cannot provide the reference). Picture yourself on Calvary, observing Jesus being tortured. You are close enough for Jesus to hear you, so you ask – "Jesus, how much do you love me?" With one hand already nailed to the cross, He boldly stretches the other arm as far as He can so it too can be nailed, and replies – "How much do I love you? I love you this much."

God is first. He originates, invents and creates time itself. In Scripture, God is never passive. He speaks. He questions. He challenges. He plans. He initiates. He acts. He is always the one who loves me before I even know of Him or love Him. I am essentially the perpetual responder. *Agape*, unlike the other three natural loves, is like God in that way. *Agape* is not a receptive, responding process but an initiating, creating source. Our loving actions must be driven by our loving thoughts which in turn must originate from a loving heart. A loving heart must be a humble heart. We have the capability, but do we have the will?

Will I humbly choose to love others and have my entire existence reflect, through my actions, the loving God in whose image I am created?

Reflection

Some Thoughts on the Impact of Moral Relativism

Do not conform yourselves to this age but be transformed by the renewal of your mind, that you may discern what is the will of God, what is good and pleasing and perfect. (Romans 12:2)

Peter Kreeft, as mentioned in other reflections, is one of my favorite contemporary spiritual writers. Reading his work makes my brain hurt, my heart yearn, and my conscience wince. I was introduced to Kreeft about 20 years ago by Msgr. Richard Lopez who has taught at St. Pius Catholic X High School in Atlanta for several decades. Msgr. Lopez had a genuinely positive spiritual influence on both of our children, who were blessed to be taught by him while attending St. Pius. I had delivered a day-long, in-service training session for the faculty and as a "thank you," Msgr. Lopez gave me a copy of Kreeft's book, *Making Choices – Finding Black and White in a World of Grays*. From the outset, I was struck by Kreeft's argument that if we are to survive in today's world and get to heaven, we must accept the reality that our loving God gave us a clear set of moral absolutes, truths that we must abide by. Living our lives by doing what feels good, doing whatever we want to do, justifying each of our choices, rationalizing our behavior so that we can live and let live, comes with consequences. Just like in Newton's third law of motion in physics, "to every action there is always an equal and opposed reaction," when

155

we choose to make choices contrary to God's design for our well being, there are consequences, logical consequences that we must suffer.

Moral relativism is a philosophy that asserts there is no global, absolute moral law that applies to all people, for all time, and in all places. Instead of an objective moral law, it espouses a *qualified* view where morals are concerned, especially in the areas of individual moral practice where personal and situational encounters supposedly dictate the correct moral position. Summing up the relative moral philosophy, Frederick Nietzsche wrote, "You have your way, I have my way. As for the right way, the correct way, it does not exist." For those who may not be familiar with Friedrich Nietzsche, he was a well-known late 19th century German philosopher who spent his energy challenging the foundations of Christianity and traditional morality.

Modern society has developed moral relativism into an art form. We see it every day. We are often numb to it. We likely fall prey to it. We likely promote some aspects of it, without even knowing it. Our education system is full of it, both public and private, including Catholic schools. Moral relativism is alive and well in our public policies, our politics, our writing (and rewriting) of history, and our treatment of each other including how we treat the poor and helpless. Our legal system is full of it. Our families are exposed to it almost everywhere they turn. The written and broadcast media rub our noses into it on a near constant basis. Their assault and the assault of politicians and bureaucrats come in a variety of forms; for example, a lack of willingness to tell the truth (or the full truth) either because it is not convenient or it does not meet the outlet's political objectives. There really are moral absolutes (murder really is murder, even if committed by someone who had a difficult childhood). The silliness goes on, nearly nonstop. Just listen to the conversation on most news broadcasts (regardless the outlet), most political interviews or even neighbors talking to one another. What havoc moral relativism has reeked on our lives.

In their wonderfully informative book, *The Real Story – Understanding the Big Picture of the Bible*, Edward Sri and Curtis Martin provide a healthy and helpful perspective:

> When a culture views religion as "just a bunch of rules," and morality as the Church "trying to tell others what to do with their lives," it no longer sees the moral law as coming from the heart of a loving father who wants what is best for us. Like Adam and Eve, our modern world has not just abandoned moral truth; it has bought into the serpent's lie about God Himself.

As much as we might want to believe otherwise, waves break against rocky coastlines, not the other way around. We crash ourselves against the very guidelines that ensure our eternal happiness with God as opposed to those guidelines beating us over the head. Why do we (I) insist on doing that? Blessed John Henry Newman was "spot on" when he observed: "We can believe what we choose, (but) we are answerable for what we choose to believe." Very simply, there are consequences to our choices.

In schools today, of paramount importance is the concept of guarding children's "self-esteem." And while that issue is important, how many absurd ways has that fundamentally meaningful concept been played out. For example, this past spring, a number of high schools chose not to have the traditional valedictory or salutatory addresses by the best and brightest of the senior class, because singling them out might make others feel bad! Really? So some students work their fingers to the bone, doing their work, doing it well, turning it in on time, and we fear that others might be offended because the diligent students are recognized for their efforts?

Another example played out recently in Colorado where the parents of a 6-year old boy, who preferred to think of himself as a girl, insisted their son be permitted to use the girl's bath room.

Slightly more than forty years ago, the Supreme Court of the United States, the highest judicial body in the land, came down on the side of a mother's right to decide whether or not the baby she carried could live or die, with millions of babies being legally murdered as a result. Obviously, to the Justices who decided on this case, a mother's right to not have a baby was far more important than the inalienable rights of the defenseless baby in her womb. About Roe v. Wade, Mother Teresa said simply (everything she said, she said that way), "When a mother can kill her baby, what is left of civilization to save?"

Peter Kreeft tells of a doctor he knows who spent two years working in the Congo to win the trust and confidence of the native people so he could eventually help them understand how their diet was killing them. Once that trust was established, those people, whom some would call primitive, asked him about America. He told them there were people who did not believe in God (to their astonishment) and that there were over a million mothers per year who paid doctors to kill their babies before they were born (to their total disbelief). They had no way of even comprehending those realities of our society. We have no way to comprehend either do we? Or do we?

Quoting from Kreeft's, *How to Win the Culture War*:

> If the God of life does not respond to this culture of death with judgment, then God is not God. If God does not honor the blood of the hundreds of millions of innocent victims of this culture of death, then the God of the Bible, the God of Abraham, the God of Israel, the God of the prophets, the God of orphans

and widows, the Defender of the defenseless, is a man-made myth, a fairy tale, an ideal as insubstantial as a dream.

Continuing, Kreeft says:

But (you may object) is not the God of the Bible merciful and forgiving? He is indeed. But the unrepentant refuse forgiveness. And forgiveness, being a gift, must be freely given and freely received. How can it be received by a moral relativist who denies that there is anything to forgive except unforgiveness, nothing to judge but judgmentalism? How can a Pharisee or pop psychologist be saved?

Let's be clear. We are in a cultural war. But that cultural war is not really between Christians and Muslims, or Catholics and Protestants, or any other pair of obvious combatants. Our cultural war is between the cultural of life and the culture of death.

In a post Patriots' Day Boston Marathon bombing interview about the Tsarnaev brothers, the uncle of those young men commented to reporters that his two nephews brought shame on their country of Kazakhstan, their culture, their family, their parents, and themselves. In hearing that statement, it occurred to me that I have not heard any public debate or even conversation about *shame* for a very long time, possibly decades. Most of the time, when someone does something wrong, the idea of shame for the wrongdoing is seldom mentioned. Instead, we prefer to do what is politically correct, and gloss over issues because we certainly would not want to impinge on someone's self-esteem. No doubt the action of those two young men was caused by some misguided sense of loyalty or patriotism, some unfortunate parentage, some bad company, whatever. In fact, it is really simple to rationalize almost anything we want to justify, particularly when there is no litmus test or standard against which we can compare. To be sure, there are moral standards; there are moral absolutes. There are both black and white. There is right – and there is wrong.

Even the term "self-esteem" no longer carries its original meaning. According to Timothy Radcliff, former Master of the worldwide Dominican Order, *self-esteem* used to be the major part of the definition of humility. Humility is truthfully looking at ourselves, recognizing the gifts God gave us, and using those gifts to serve the legitimate needs of others. Now, in the loosest form, self-esteem is simply feeling good about oneself, regardless. But just because something feels good does not make it right, or even okay. The idea that I should be ashamed of myself for having done something wrong, for having sinned, for having violated a moral absolute seems to have vanished because of the moral relativist mentality. How or why should I be ashamed of doing something wrong, when I am fully free to justify virtually anything I do? Besides, shame does not feel good, so why should I inflict that upon myself. For Catholics, this notion creates quite a conundrum, especially in light of our Sacrament of Reconciliation.

Church teaching says that we must examine our consciences, admit to ourselves and to God that we have done wrong, be fully sorry for having done the wrong, confess those wrongs to a priest and promise to strive not to do that wrong again. Recite the Act of Contrition out loud, regardless which version you normally say (if you do not know the prayer, just Google it). The essence of our beliefs about forgiveness is there, in very simple terms. Only after we have confessed and been given absolution can we legitimately begin to feel good. But the good feeling comes from the healing touch of God, not from some misconstrued sense of "I'm okay, you're okay." For those who are non-Catholic (and not blessed with access to the Sacrament of Reconciliation), forgiveness for having done wrong, regardless the act, may be as simple as humbly admitting the wrong, sincerely asking God for His forgiveness, and genuinely being sorry for the wrong, with full intent not to repeat the wrongdoing. God does not want to punish us, He wants to cherish us and He does so with an unconditional love beyond our understanding, regardless the sin(s) we may have committed. For those who may feel there is no hope for them, just ask for forgiveness and forgiveness will be granted!

I was blessed to have been raised by wonderful, loving parents and clearly remember my Dad counseling me and my two siblings that each time we looked into the mirror, we better be able to respect the person looking back at us. In his own way, my dad was asking us to examine the image in the mirror and ask the questions, "Can I respect you? Are my actions consistent with what I say I believe? Are my actions consistent with moral absolutes? Am I worthy of trust?" His challenge *was* a challenge. And I must admit, on far more than one occasion, I had to truthfully answer that I did not respect the person looking back at me from the mirror. Those occasions were (and frankly still are) calls to action. Straighten up. Get your act together. Receive the Sacrament of Reconciliation. Get back on the right track. What simple, yet profound advice. My dad was a wonderful model of integrity for my siblings and me.

In Psalm 36: 2-5, David writes eloquently:

Sin directs the heart of the wicked man; his eyes are closed to the fear of God. For he lives with the delusion: his guilt will not be known and hated. Empty and false are the words of his mouth; he has ceased to be wise and do good. On his bed he hatches plots; he sets out on a wicked way; he does not reject evil.

David spoke not from a position of observing and criticizing others, rather he spoke from examining his own heart.

Matthew 23:27-32 records a strong rebuke by Jesus of the religious leaders of his own time. In the first two of seven such warnings:

> *Jesus said, "Woe to you, scribes and Pharisees, you hypocrites. You are like whitewashed tombs, which appear beautiful on the outside, but inside are full of dead men's bones and every kind of filth. Even so, on the outside you appear righteous, but inside you are filled with hypocrisy and evildoing. Woe to you, scribes and Pharisees, you hypocrites. You build the tombs of the prophets and adorn the memorials of the righteous, and you say, "If we had lived in the days of our ancestors, we would not have joined them in shedding the prophets' blood." Thus you bear witness against yourselves that you are the children of those who murdered the prophets; now fill up what your ancestors measured out!"*

Would it not be easy to look at these externally pious people and wonder how they could have such despicable cores? Of course it would, but doing so would be hypocritical. Russian writer Aleksandr Solzhenitsyn said, the dividing line between good and evil doesn't pass through parties, groups, or classes of people. "It cuts through the heart of every human being." The wiser choice would be to be far more attentive to the image in the mirror, because, very frankly, there is a bit of Pharisee in each of us. We would be well served by being truthful about our faults and working hard to correct them rather than covering them up to create a positive impression with others. I recently read a meditation in *The Word Among Us* that observed:

But blessed be God, who never stops loving us and

calling us out of these tombs we have constructed for ourselves! Whenever we turn to Him, He gives us the courage to search our hearts, the humility to confess our sins, and the grace to take another step into the light of Christ. As we do, He doesn't only help us to shed our sins – He makes us into the very "aroma of Christ," spreading "the odor of the knowledge of Him" everywhere we go (2 Corinthians 2:14-15).

There are moral absolutes and they were given to us by a God who loves us and wants us to share eternity with Him. While ignoring those truths might result in some sort of immediate pleasure, such pleasure fades rapidly. God's plan for our joy and happiness comes when we align ourselves with the rules of the road He provided. Only then will we be equipped to fully live humbly and to graciously serve all those we touch in this life.

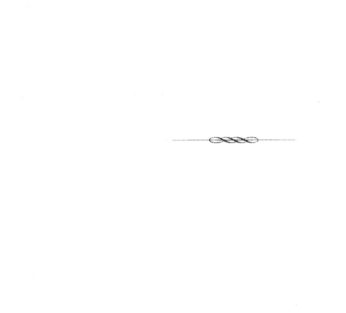

With That Their Eyes Were Opened

*With that their eyes were opened and they recognized
him, but he vanished from their sight. (Luke 24:31)*

Scripture readings for daily Mass offer truly remarkable
insights into how we are to live and love. For example,
the gospel reading for daily mass a few days after Easter
is Luke 24:13-35, the story of the Road to Emmaus. In that
familiar narrative, Jesus approached two men walking from
Jerusalem to Emmaus. They were talking feverishly about
the events of the weekend, particularly what had happened
during the early hours of that first Easter Sunday. The men
could not believe that anyone, even in an age where virtually
all communication and news transmission was by word of
mouth, could not know what had happened to Jesus the
Nazarean. But Jesus, whom the men did not recognize, made
them think He did not know and asked them to tell Him.
The men explained in detail the series of events that took
place. Then they added that they (and many others of Jesus'
followers) had been so very certain that Jesus would be the
one to redeem Israel, but now they did not know what they
were to believe. He died. Yet apparently He had risen from
the dead! Clearly the enormity of all that had happened had
overcome them.

Jesus said to them:

*Oh, how foolish you are! How slow of heart to believe
all that the prophets spoke! Was it not necessary that
the Messiah should suffer these things and enter into
his glory? (Luke 24:25)*

He then interpreted scripture for them beginning with Moses
and the prophets. What must they have been thinking and
feeling? Might the situation have been similar to what
the elders thought and felt while listening to the 12-year
old Jesus teaching in the temple during the time He was
separated from Mary and Joseph? The Master Teacher was
being listened to with intensity, but the listeners' ears were
closed and their eyes were veiled – they could not see that
He was the Messiah, the Son of the living God.

Still unaware of His identity, the travelers convinced
Jesus to stick around, eat with them and spend the night. For
some reason, they simply knew they wanted to spend more
time with Him. But in verses 30-31, Luke reports:

*And it happened that, while he was with them at table,
he took bread, said the blessing, broke it, and gave
it to them. With that their eyes were opened and they
recognized him, but he vanished from their sight.*

"With that their eyes were opened and they recognized him."

Jesus had been in their midst while they walked for what
must have been several hours. They talked about Him, and
there He was, and they did not know He was with them.
Is that not how we can be much of the time? We are able
to see circumstances and people around us but do not see
Jesus in those people or those events. In fact, we often miss
the obvious opportunities to be Jesus to those that are the
closest to us – our spouse, our children and grandchildren,
our neighbors. Is it possible that we simply do not see?

To love and serve one another is what we are called to do
as Christians. To speak the truth to one another in all things

is what we are obligated to do as Christians. To be good stewards of our time, talent and treasure is how we must live as Christians. Yet events and personalities can be, in a very real way, cataracts that cloud both how and what we see.

The Monday before Easter this past year, on our back porch, my wife and I were doing our normal morning prayers, Liturgy of the Hours – Morning Prayers, daily mass readings, meditation on the mass readings from *The Word Among Us*, etc. We were anxiously awaiting the arrival of our daughter and three grandchildren for a four-day spring-break visit.

The gospel reading was John 12:1-44, the story of Jesus' trip back to Bethany where He had raised Lazarus from the dead. Mary, Martha and Lazarus gave a dinner for Him, and of course Martha served. During the evening,

> *Mary took a liter of costly perfumed oil made from genuine aromatic nard and anointed the feet of Jesus and dried them with her hair; the house was filled with the fragrance of the oil.*

Judas boldly asked why the oil was not sold for three hundred days' wages and the money given to the poor? Of course he asked this, not because he cared about the poor, but because he was a thief and held the money bag and used to steal the contributions.

Jesus said,

> *Leave her alone. Let her keep this for the day of my burial. You always have the poor with you, but you do not always have me.*

In a different but very real way, Jesus, in this story too, removed the cataracts and cleared the cloudiness from the eyes of all those present and as usual put things into their proper perspective.

167

The reflection from "The Word Among Us" on this reading was quite interesting and revealing. I am choosing to quote much of it here because I found it so meaningful.

Does it not seem odd that Jesus would start the final week of His earthly life by attending a dinner party? You might have expected Jesus, with good reason, to have spent extra time in prayer and conversation with His Father, or in some other way strengthening Himself for the ordeal ahead. But no, He had dinner with His friends. He received their generosity and love. And He loved them back by spending time with them even at a time when more important things might have weighed heavily on Him.

All the while, Judas had his eye out for the main chance – his opportunity to skim more out of the money bag he held for Jesus and His friends. Jesus knew it, but He didn't address it when Judas rebuked Mary. He was more focused on affirming Mary's act of adoration than calling out Judas' greed. Evidently, Mary's love was more significant than Judas' selfishness.

Isn't this amazing? Even as Jesus approached the hour of His death, His focus was on love: Loving others, receiving the love they offered Him. Corrections, weaknesses – even sin – took a backseat to love.

Don't forget about sin, but try to focus on love this Holy Week. Take Mary's example and be extravagant in how you express your love for God and for those around you. Spend the week sowing patience and reconciliation when you find yourself in situations that aggravate you. Show forbearance when sharp or cutting remarks rise in your thoughts during the day. Offer forgiveness – quietly, unseen, even unasked or unspoken. Think of an act of service or affirmation you could do for someone. Maybe even host a dinner party for friends!

And of course, spend time with Jesus, pouring out on Him that which is most precious to you. If you are a habitually busy person, offer Him some one-on-one time. Whether it involves time or money, praise or service, think of a way to *love extravagantly* this week. Be creative as you consider how you can shift your focus, and ask the Holy Spirit to give you ideas that make the most sense for you. Above all, love others as deeply as you can, for love covers a multitude of sins.

For those who have young children or grandchildren, you know they can be very loud, energetic, and sometimes nerve-wracking. Our three grandchildren certainly are. But the challenging statement about loving extravagantly hit my wife and me right between the eyes. What a wonderful vision of how we (or should I say I) need to treat them, particularly when they are rowdy – *love them extravagantly*. My eyes were opened, the cataracts were removed – and I was able to see the wonderful way God had spoken to us through that passage.

As their grandfather, I clearly have responsibility to keep them safe and to ensure that they followed the rules – but I could do all those things, including being the 'enforcer' and still love them extravagantly, treating them with calm and kindness. I must say that our commitment to *love extravagantly* during our time together made everyone's lives a lot more fun and enjoyable. Did the grandchildren push our buttons? Absolutely! But we were able to shower them with love in a way that was similar to the way Jesus' friend, Mary, shared her love for Jesus by anointing Him. In fact, Laurel and I have spoken often since then about loving

169

extravagantly. No doubt you know of situations in which you, too, must dig deep in order to love extravagantly.

The image of having our eyes opened to see clearly (or see more clearly) was depicted in at least two other daily mass readings that same week, specifically, stories from the early chapters of the Acts of the Apostles, stories of events in the immediate aftermath of the Resurrection.

The first such story that St. Luke provides is of Peter speaking to the crowd on the first Pentecost. The Spirit took the words that Peter spoke and brought them to life in the hearts of those in the crowd. By the power of the Spirit, the people realized that Peter's words were true. Jesus really was Messiah and Lord. His resurrection really had ushered in a new age for Israel (for mankind). The kingdom had come, and they were being invited to enter it! Moved by Peter's words and the Spirit's work, the people all responded with one voice in Acts 2:37: *"What are we to do?"* They were touched so deeply (and parenthetically had their eyes opened) that three thousand of them became followers of Jesus that day. The response to Peter's discourse was far more than a quick emotional reaction to a moving sermon. For each of those three thousand converts, the response was a fundamental change of heart that resulted in changed lives! They saw things clearly, in a way they had never seen them before. We have a similar opportunity each day as we read and meditate on Scripture.

Jesus wants us to listen for the urgings of the Holy Spirit as we read so the words come alive in our hearts as well. He wants to move us to ask: "What should I do? How do you want me to respond to your word today?" Jesus wants our eyes to be open so that our hearts will be open, so that our minds will be enlightened, so that we will be moved to serve others humbly and with generosity.

When our eyes are opened we may be able see sinfulness in ourselves that we need to confess. We may be moved

170

to sing a song of praise or to pray for a specific need for a loved one. We may even be moved to share with someone how our faith has helped us through a difficult time in our life. Whatever you think the Spirit is saying as your eyes are opened, try to act on it while the conviction is still strong.

In a second story the same week, soon after Pentecost, Peter and John approached the gate of the temple where they encountered a crippled man pleading to them for whatever few coins they might have. The apostles, in reply, let the poor man know they had nothing of earthly value, but within a few minutes the cripple arose and walked – he had been cured. The people who saw what happened hurried in amazement toward Peter and John. Peter, in what must have been a bit of frustration, said to them (Acts 3:12-18):

> *You Israelites, why are you amazed at this, and why do you look so intently at us as if we had made him walk by our own power or piety? The God of Abraham, the God of Isaac, and the God of Jacob, the God of our ancestors, has glorified his servant Jesus whom you handed over and denied in Pilate's presence, when he had decided to release him. You denied the Holy and Righteous One and asked that a murderer be released to you. The author of life you put to death, but God raised him from the dead; of this we are witnesses. And by faith in his name, this man, whom you see and know, his name has made strong, and the faith that comes through it has given him this perfect health, in the presence of all of you. Now I know, brothers, that you acted out of ignorance, just as your leaders did; but God has thus brought to fulfillment what he had announced beforehand through the mouth of all the prophets, that his Messiah would suffer.*

Peter then reminded them:

> *Moreover, all the prophets who spoke, from Samuel and those afterwards, also announced these days. You are the children of the prophets and of the covenant that God made with your ancestors when he said to Abraham, "In your offspring all the families of the earth shall be blessed." For you first, God raised up his servant and sent him to bless you by turning each of you from your evil ways. (Acts 3:24-26)*

Their eyes were opened! They already knew what the prophets had said, but did not understand – *but now they saw.*

During my second mission trip to Honduras several years ago, I experienced a dramatic opening of my eyes while listening to a homily entitled, "Aggressive Humility." More clearly than ever before, the Holy Spirit allowed me to see and understand that true leadership, the kind of leadership we are all called to demonstrate in all aspects of our lives, is a passionate dedication to the unconditional loving service of others. What a wonderful way to love extravagantly.

> *How will your eyes be opened today?*
> *How will you love extravagantly, particularly those you have been called to serve?*

Reflection

Defending, Extending, and Caring for the Faith

*The LORD God then called to the man and asked
him: "Where are you?" He answered, "I heard you
in the garden; but I was afraid, because I was naked,
so I hid." Then God asked: "Who told you that you
were naked? Have you eaten from the tree of which
I had forbidden you to eat?" The man replied, "The
woman whom you put here with me – she gave me
fruit from the tree, so I ate it." The LORD God then
asked the woman: "What is this you have done?" The
woman answered, "The snake tricked me, so I ate it."*
(Genesis 3:9-12)

And so began mankind's relationship with our Creator and
loving God. From nearly the beginning we have been duped
into doing what we were told not to do, blaming others when
we did, and so on. And, unfortunately, we have been in a
similar struggle throughout our existence. On the merciful
side, however, God sent the Holy Spirit to guide us and help
strengthen our often faltering faith through sanctifying grace
so we can withstand temptations and attacks of all sorts.

Pope Benedict XVI, in an Apostolic Letter, *Porta Fidei*
(2011), declared a *Year of Faith* beginning October 11, 2012,
concluding on November 24, 2013. The first day of the *Year of
Faith*, commemorated the fiftieth anniversary of the opening
of the Second Vatican Council and the twentieth anniversary
of the publication of the *Catechism of the Catholic Church.*

The *Year of Faith* was intended to be an opportunity for Catholics to experience a conversion – to turn back to Jesus and enter into a deeper relationship with Him. The "door of faith" is opened at our baptism, but during this year we were called to open it again, walk through it and rediscover and renew our relationship with Christ and His Church.

The Pope's declaration was no accident, and frankly could not have come at a more important time, not only for our country – but for the rest of the world as well. I would like to share a few thoughts about why I think the *Year of Faith* was so very important to defend, extend and care for our faith.

At a meeting of the Pontifical Academy in 2010, a think tank founded in 1994 by Pope John Paul II, scholars from around the world reported on a wide range of research related to religious freedoms. Harvard professor of Law, Mary Ann Glendon, a member of the Academy and participant at the 2010 meeting, reported on some of the proceedings from the Academy at a talk she gave at Emory University's Aquinas Center of Theology. According to Glendon, possibly the most startling issues reported on at the meeting were indications that less value is being attached to religion and religious freedom in places where she would have hoped it would be most secure – in the minds and hearts of citizens of liberal democracies, including the United States.

A recent study by the Pew Forum on Religion and Public Life (2012, *Rising Time of Restrictions on Religion*) reported nearly seventy percent of the world's people live in countries where there are high restrictions on religious freedom due to governmental policies or social hostilities or both. Not surprisingly, the brunt of these restrictions falls on religious minorities. Worldwide, to the surprise of many, seventy-five percent of the victims of violent religious persecution are *Christians*.

In another recent survey, the Eurobarometer Poll (2010), conducted by the European Union, slightly more than half of Europeans say that they believe in God, although another quarter of the population say they believe in a "spirit" or "life force." Still another survey (European Values Survey, 2010) showed that when given a list of twelve 'values' and asked to pick the three that they considered most important, only seven percent of Europeans listed religion. Forty-six percent said they thought religion plays too important a place in society – a rather remarkable and disturbing shift toward secularism.

Fortunately, results from similar studies in the United States are far less dramatic – ninety-two percent say they believe in God or some sort of universal spirit, and a majority of those polled said that religion is very important in their lives. Troubling, though, an increasing proportion of Americans (sixteen percent) decline to affiliate with any organized religion and between eighteen and thirty-three percent describe themselves as spiritual instead of religious, indicating a growing disillusionment with organized religion. Possibly more troubling are the results of the Pew Forum's survey of young Americans between the ages of eighteen and twenty-nine indicating they are considerably less religious than previous generations at the same age. While young adults have historically taken sabbaticals from the practice of their faith, particularly during their college and early adult years, surveys indicate that currently fewer are actively practicing their faith than in the past.

In her presentation at Emory, Professor Glendon further commented that, "since the 1940's, Supreme Court majorities have tended to treat religion as primarily an affair between the individual and his or her God. These rulings have given short shrift not only to the vast number of Americans for whom the existence of a worshiping community is essential to religious experience but also to the social settings where religious "beliefs and practices are generated, regenerated, nurtured...and transmitted from one generation to the next."

With the growing mobility of and growing decay of family life, we are continually challenged in passing on our faith to generations coming along behind us.

Attacks on our religious freedoms have materialized in a myriad of ways in recent years. For example, in 2006, Catholic Charities in the Boston Archdiocese (Catholic News Service, March 13, 2006) chose to close down its adoption services rather than mount a full-scale legal battle against state licensing requirements that would have prevented their agency from operating in a manner consistent with Catholic teaching about marriage. On another front, recent regulations originally issued by the U.S. Department of Health and Human Services related to Affordable Care Act define "religious employer" so narrowly as to effectively deny conscience protection to most groups who would wish to claim them. And, prospects that religiously affiliated, nonprofit hospitals may be required to choose between shutting down and providing services that violate their religious beliefs still loom. Recent rulings by the Supreme Court of the United States, however, have provided exemptions for a larger class of employers who have religious objections to the mandates related to birth control and abortions.

Even though I have briefly described only two examples here, the list of similar situations is getting longer by the day. We could easily conclude that our society, our legal system, our legislative bodies are waging an all-out attack on those of us who wish to practice our faith and support true freedom of religion, as opposed to freedom from religion. As a reminder, the *First Amendment* clearly states that: *Congress shall make no law respecting an establishment of religion, or prohibiting the free exercise thereof.* Dr. Glendon, in her presentation makes a convincing case that freedom of religion is, for all practical purposes, being relegated to the status of a second-class right. If this surprises you, just think back over the past few years how many times the courts

176

seem to have given freedom of speech trump-card status over freedom of religion.

And the silliness (or should I say insanity) continues. The ACLU of North Carolina's Legal Foundation filed a lawsuit in the U.S. District Court for the Eastern District of North Carolina in September, 2011. The suit was filed on behalf of North Carolinians seeking a specialty license plate that supports a "woman's right to reproductive freedom," in direct response to a previous request by pro-life groups who had requested a "Choose Life" license plate be offered. The federal judge ruled in November, 2012, that "The State's offering of a 'Choose Life' license plate in the absence of a pro-choice plate constitutes viewpoint discrimination in violation of the First Amendment." I personally find a great deal of irony in the notion that a state would actually want to defend the right to kill a baby before it takes its first breath. If we are willing to issue license plates promoting abortion, why not issue some endorsing capital punishment, or euthanasia? Just because abortion is currently legal in our country does not make it right. The "Choose Life" message, very simply, is about promoting the dignity of life in all ways. The rest is details.

Interestingly, the attacks we currently face on our faith and religious freedoms are remarkably similar to what went on during the French Revolution in the late seventeenth century. Religious irreverence became so fashionable among French elites that they managed to propagate that irreverence to the lower classes. Religion began to be replaced by a wide range of loyalties and secular ideas that significantly threatened those who remained loyal to the practice of their faith.

As easy as it might be to say, the faith challenges we face are not just from external source – they are often from our own personal doing. One such significant interruption is technology. Our daily lives are ruled by it. No doubt you have, already today, been exposed to numerous technological events, and likely you are mostly unaware of them – alarm clock, hot water, indoor plumbing, cars, traffic lights, electricity – shall I continue? Are your cell phones, smart phones, etc. interruptions, distractions, or direct challenges to living your faith?

My friend, Phil Thompson, Director of the Aquinas Center of Theology at Emory University recently published a book entitled, *Returning to Reality – Thomas Merton's Wisdom for a Technological World*. Merton was a world-renowned Trappist philosopher and author of more than 60 books. Writing from his monastic home in Gethsemane, Kentucky, 50 years ago, Merton commented:

> We would like to be quiet, but our restlessness will not allow it. Hence we believe that for us there can be no peace except in a life filled up with movement and activity, with speech, news, communication, recreation, and distraction. We seek the meaning of our life in activity for its own sake, activity without objective, efficacy without fruit, scientism, the cult of unlimited power, the service of the machine as end in itself.

Interesting observation, particularly in light of the fact it was made a full half century ago.

But recognition of the dangers of being enticed by external distractions goes further back than Thomas Merton. Four centuries before the birth of Christ, nearly two and a half millennia ago, Taoist philosopher Chuang Tzu, in a poem entitled "The Inner Law", wrote:

> He who is controlled by objects
> Loses possession of his inner self.
> If he no longer values himself,
> How can he value others?

178

If he no longer values others,
He is abandoned.
He has nothing left!

In *Disputed Questions*, Merton observed:

Those who seek to build a better world without God
are those who, trusting in money, power, technology
and organization deride the spiritual strength of faith
and love and fix all their hopes on a huge monolithic
society, having a monopoly over all power, all
production, and even over the minds of its members.
But to alienate the spirit of man by subjecting him
to such monstrous indignity is to make injustice and
violence inevitable.

Less than an hour before I heard the news of the
Columbine High School shootings on April 20, 1999, I read
for the first time, these words from Lee Bolman and Terry
Deal's book, *Leading with Soul*:

Disease of the soul exacts a high price. Spiritual
bankruptcy ultimately leads to economic failure.
The deeper cost is the world where everything has
function yet nothing has meaning. The symptoms
of an undernourished soul appear in countless
ways: violence, lethargy, alienation, alcoholism,
deterioration of the family.

The memory of the juxtaposition of those words and the
events of the day are indelibly burned into my memory.

Often times we might be lulled into believing that our
faith alone will keep us safe. But Merton observed:

The (Catholic) faith (is) "not a kind of radio electric eye which is meant to assess the state of our neighbor's conscience." Instead we should envision faith as a "need by which we draw the thread of charity through our neighbor's soul and sew ourselves together in one Christ." (But) This binding of humanity in charity must begin with a spiritual connection or it would lose its bearings.

In other words, Merton encourages us to look for a significant amount of our strength by being in community with others struggling with the challenges of life, just like we are.

But simply being in community is not enough, because, as Merton cautions:

The transformation of society begins within the person. It begins with the maturing and opening of our personal freedom in relation to other freedoms – in relation to the rest of society. The Christian "giving" that is required of us is full and intelligent participation in the life of our world, not only on a basis of natural law but also in the communion and reconciliation of interpersonal love. This means a capacity to be open to others as persons, to desire for others all that we know to be needful for ourselves, all this required for the full growth and even the temporal happiness of a fully personal existence.

But frankly, all of this can be an overwhelming challenge. We have so many demands on our time, talent and treasure. How can we possibly juggle all of the competing demands? In fact, such competition goes to the heart of our human condition, just like joy and sorrow do. Henri J. M. Nouwen, Dutch-born Catholic priest and spiritual author, in his book, *Can You Drink the Cup*, addresses this issue:

The cup of life is the cup of joy as much as it is the cup of sorrow. Mourning and dancing are never separates. If joys could not be where sorrows are, the cup of life would never be drinkable. That is why we have to hold the cup in our hands and look carefully to see the joys hidden in our sorrows.

What many of us do not seem to know or understand is that Jesus' kingdom is already here. That kingdom arrived the day He was born, and it replaced the kingdom of the world on the day He died for us. Evidence of this reality for each of us happened at Pentecost. A meditation from *The Word Among Us*, November 15, 2012, counsels:

Rather than focus our attention on being ready for the day when Jesus comes back, maybe we should focus on all those people who still haven't embraced the kingdom that He has already inaugurated. For when Jesus said: "The kingdom of God is among you," He wasn't pointing only to Himself. He meant us as well. How does it feel knowing that you are a sign of the kingdom of God? Yes, in your frail humanity, you carry within you the new life that Jesus now lives in heaven. Whether or not you even know it, you have the ability to live for "the praise of the glory of His grace." That's what baptism did for you. If you want to know the power of this kingdom, the answer is both easy and life-consuming: Fix your eyes on Jesus, not your weaknesses and faults.

While our faith journey is deeply personal, that journey cannot be taken alone. In many ways we need to follow the example of John the Baptist who spent his ministry near the Jordan, preaching the need to be baptized and to repent for our sins. He readily admitted that he was "A voice of one crying out in the desert" and that we must each "Prepare the way of the Lord, make straight his path." The way is not easy. St. Paul in his letter to the Ephesians 6:11-17, however encourages us to prepare this way:

> *Put on the armor of God so that you may be able to stand firm against the tactics of the devil. For our struggle is not with flesh and blood but with the principalities, with the powers, with the world rulers of this present darkness, with the evil spirits in the heavens. Therefore, put on the armor of God that you may be able to resist on the evil day and, having done everything, to hold your ground. So stand fast with your loins girded in truth, clothed with righteousness as a breastplate, and your feet shod in readiness for the gospel of peace. In all circumstances, hold faith as a shield, to quench all [the] flaming arrows of the evil one. And take the helmet of salvation and the sword of the Spirit, which is the word of God.*

Let's keep the faith, Brothers and Sisters, and defend and care for it with all our strength!

Reflection

XXI

The Courage to Serve

*I am the good shepherd. The good shepherd lays
down his life for the sheep. (John 10:11)*

In science and history, using more than one approach to
independently confirm a theory or conclusion is usually
referred to as building multiple or converging lines of
evidence. Theologians and Scripture scholars also strive to
develop multiple lines of evidence as they try to understand
or make sense of events and words that often are quite
confusing or mysterious. During the past several weeks,
I experienced a swirl of converging lines of evidence or
thoughts leading to this reflection. Those multiple and
seemingly independent suggestions came from news reports
of the day (particularly about numerous situations in the
Middle East and Africa), from an email, a You-Tube video,
a homily, and from multiple liturgical events and scripture
passages taken from ceremonies of Holy Week. "Just how
important is courage to serving God in ways that God wants
to be served?"

I was reminded recently, by way of a mass email from
the Dynamic Catholic, about Saint Maximilian Kolbe,
one of our inspirational modern-day saints. He was a
true testament of courage in the service of others. Kolbe
was a Polish Catholic priest imprisoned at the Auschwitz
concentration camp during World War II. His crime was
nothing more than being a Catholic priest. Three prisoners

escaped from the camp not long after he arrived, so to deter other prisoners from attempting escape, the commanding officers decided to randomly select ten men to starve to death in an underground bunker. One of the selected ten cried out, "My wife! My children!" Upon hearing the man's plea, Father Kolbe volunteered to take his place, and was allowed to do so. After two weeks of no food and water, Kolbe was the only one still alive. By this time, though, the guards were bored and wanted to be done with the exercise, so they administered a lethal injection to get rid of him. Did Kolbe know that he was going to die when he volunteered to take that pleading father's place? I believe he did. He chose to courageously give up his own life in hopes that the dad would be spared to care for his family even though he knew he himself would die.

1 John 3:16 comes to mind:

The way we came to know love was that he laid down his life for us; so we ought to lay down our lives for our brothers.

What a beautiful reminder of what Jesus did for us on Good Friday.

In a chapter in my first book, entitled "When the Going Gets Tough," I related the story of a disabled Viet Nam veteran I was honored to meet at Dulles Airport, while waiting for a delayed flight back to Atlanta from a business trip. During the course of our conversation, I found myself asking Bill about his injuries, his military service experiences, and his current situation. Bill had served in Viet Nam, had been injured numerous times by gunfire and Claymore mine explosions, had been contaminated with Agent Orange, had experienced napalm, and had been shot more times than he could remember. His exposure to Agent Orange eventually led to his developing type-II diabetes, which in turn led to kidney failure and the need for a kidney transplant.

Bill told me about having seen *We Were Soldiers* (a movie reported to be one of the most realistic depictions of experiences by our military in Viet Nam) and being able to smell the napalm during scenes showing its use. He could remember being able to "see" the white streaks made by bullets cutting through the humid, jungle air. I expected at any moment to begin hearing venomous comments about his disabilities, chronic health issues, or his lot in life, but none came.

Bill related that not long after he returned to the United States, he learned that he had diabetes moments before he was about to make still another jump as a member of the 82nd Airborne with a full 110-pound complement of gear on his back. Just as he was about to jump, he passed out and fell out of the plane unconscious. Fortunately for Bill, his jumpmaster saw him fall and immediately dove, head-first, out of the plane after him, caught up with him, pulled his rip cord, and saved his life. Sometime later, additional military service injuries cost him his hands and the ability to walk. Bill's candor and lack of anger at his fate struck me as amazing. If anyone had the right to feel sorry for himself, it was Bill. Courage, as we know, is acting in the face of fear or danger, one sign of a true leader and of a true Christian. Bill and his jumpmaster are both really courageous men putting themselves in harm's way for others in extraordinary ways.

I asked Bill what kind of work he does now and should not have been surprised at his reply, but I was. He has dedicated the rest of his life to helping others with multiple traumatic injuries like his own by becoming a minister. Bill chose a vocation fully dedicated to serving those with whom he crosses paths. What a beautiful and courageous response to being handed a very heavy cross to bear.

In a similarly holy and heroic manner as demonstrated by St. Maximillian Kolbe during World War II, another saintly 'Servant of God' arose during our country's involvement in

Viet Nam during the 1960's. Father Vincent Capodanno, a member of the Catholic Foreign Mission Society of America (often referred to as the Maryknolls) was a Navy Chaplain assigned to, at different times the 1st (Regiment), 5th and 7th Marines (Mode, 2000).

Following his ordination, Father Capodanno was sent to a remote part of Taiwan where he served as a missionary for a half dozen years, then relocated to Hong Kong to work in a school. While dedicated to selflessly serving God and His people in both of these assignments, he felt a strong calling to be a military chaplain. Eventually he was given permission to become a Navy Chaplain and, at his request was deployed to work with the Marines in Viet Nam. Father Capodanno was an exceptional chaplain. He lived with the men he served, he ate with them, heard their confession, administered other sacraments, and frequently patrolled dangerous perimeters and kept the marines company in jungle outposts ministering to those most in danger. They were his flock, and as their shepherd he put them at the top of his priorities, always above himself.

Father Capodanno often listened in on radio transmissions to determine the troops most in danger and hitched rides on helicopters so he could be with those men in their times of need. He was frequently seen leaping out of his helicopter taxi in the midst of battle. Because of his insistence on being with the Marines he was assigned to, he was nicknamed the Grunt Padre! In very short order, he became the most sought after chaplain in the Marine Corps. The troops he served simply loved him. He shared everything he had with them and was available to them any time of day or night. His granting of General Absolution before the Marines went into battle unburdened their consciences and instilled in them the courage to fight. Chaplain Capodanno's mere presence in a unit lifted the morale of all on patrol.

Live Humbly, Serve Graciously

Many of his 'parishioners' were demoralized as the peace protests began back home, so Capodanno made it his job to do everything he could to raise their spirits. He administered medical care to the physically wounded, and ministered to their spiritual needs by blessing them, hearing their confessions, giving communion to the Catholic service men and offering mass wherever possible. His daily routine seldom changed. Father Cap's daily routine was living out what Pope Francis's admonition (many years later) was to his priests, to live with his flock. Not surprising, when his tour of duty came to an end, he requested (and was granted) an extension.

On September 4, 1967, a helicopter carrying Father Capodanno to the site of a large-scale offensive (Operation Swift) crashed. The 5th Marines found themselves outnumbered 5-to-1 by 2,500 North Vietnamese regular troops. Although wounded twice in the course of battle early that day, he refused to be medevacked. Like a ray of hope in the midst of the storm, the Padre went up and down the line caring for the wounded and anointing the dying. During the fierce fighting, the chaplain spotted a wounded corpsman who had been hit by a burst of automatic weapon fire and was unable to move. Father Capodanno ran to his aid and began to care for his wounds. A Viet Cong machine gunner opened fire. With 27 bullet wounds in his spine, neck, and head, Father Capodanno died instantly, serving his men to the end. He gave his all and asked nothing in return.

Of the Marines he served, nearly all have said they would have happily died in his place. Father Capodanno was posthumously awarded the Congressional Medal of Honor. But even more significant than that award, his Cause for Canonization is under investigation. In this first stage toward sainthood he is called "Servant of God." Several miracles have already been attributed to invocation of his intervention, and each of those is being investigated. In the midst of that horrible and unpopular war, Father Vincent Capodanno stands out as a remarkable example of unconditional dedication of loving service to his fellow man. His ministry was marked by extraordinary courage and heroism, all for others, asking nothing in return. Father Capodanno's love and courage are on par with Saint Maximillian Kolbe in all respects.

On February 14, 2015, twenty-one Coptic Christians from Egypt were brutally martyred in Libya. These men, in Libya for jobs to earn enough money to feed their families, were forced to their knees on a beach, then beheaded, all the while being videoed with the full intent by the ISIS terrorists to use the video to shock the world. About the brutal executions, Pope Francis said, "Their only words were: 'Jesus, help me!' They were killed simply for the fact that they were Christians." Pope Francis added: "As we recall these brothers and sisters who died only because they confessed Christ, I ask that we encourage one another to go forward with this ecumenism which is giving us strength, the ecumenism of blood. The martyrs belong to all Christians." What courage those men showed, declaring the name of their Savior, knowing that all they needed to do to live was to deny Him. Their courage should serve as an example to all Christians who may be weak in their faith.

Catholics and other Christians in many parts of Iraq and Syria are also under siege – being driven from areas such as the city of Mosul, where Christians have lived for nearly two millennia. The move by Islamic extremists to eradicate Christians in the area has taken on epic proportion. Churches have been bombed, church leaders executed, children rounded up and martyred, Christian prisoners burned alive, others beheaded. Still other attacks have senselessly destroyed artifacts dating to the time of Christ – all attempts to eradicate any evidence of Christianity. Literally hundreds of thousands of Christians have been displaced, tortured or murdered simply because they courageously choose to affirm that Jesus Christ is Lord. They serve the Lord in the purest form by their willingness to accept all consequences for professing their faith. Jesus tells us in John 10:11:

> *I am the good shepherd. The good shepherd lays down his life for the sheep.*

What a remarkable living out of Jesus' example these people have demonstrated.

Another story that caught my attention recently, via YouTube, was about a Navy SEAL, Senior Chief Mike Day. His survival is what many consider a miracle. In a story from the Christian Broadcast Network, Day tells of a fire fight with Al Qaeda terrorists in 2007. He entered the doorway of a house suspected of housing members of Al Qaeda and, in his words: "Upon entering that doorway, they all just opened up on me. It felt like somebody was just beating me up with sledge-hammers. After I figured out I was getting shot at I said, 'God get me home to my girls.'" During that incident Chief Day was shot 27 times and took grenade shrapnel in a fire fight with four terrorists. He successfully took all of them down. The body armor he wore was only supposed to handle one round in a given spot before falling apart, but somehow it continued to protect him even though the gunfight happened within a range of ten feet. He took sixteen shots to the body, eleven of which were deflected by the body armor, was shot in both legs, both arms and abdomen. His comment was "You throw a finger on me, anything but my head, I got shot there." Chief Day has earned sixteen medals for his courageous service to our country. His recovery from physical injuries took more than two years, and even though he still struggles with daily pain, remarkably he chooses to deal with his situation by focusing on serving others as a Wounded Warrior advocate. He helps raise money to support a mental health facility that treats wounded veterans. Day says that the worst injuries are the ones you cannot see. He says, "My life's mission is now not about me, rather it is to care for and lead my wounded brothers and sisters. My fellow warriors deserve the best available treatment for their injuries."

Mike Day said that on the day of the attack, his prayer that he would make it home to his wife and daughters was the first real prayer he had made to God, but he firmly believes God kept him alive to do the work he is doing now.

Only a few days before Easter, 2015, 150 students at Garissa University College in Kenya were unjustly and brutally targeted and killed simply because they were Christians. Many of them were gathered for prayer but others were sought out around campus. Most were asked if they were Christian, and with their affirmative response, they died martyrs' deaths. Even though most of the students lost were not Catholic, Pope Francis, as part of his Easter address, just days after the massacre, said: "May constant prayer rise up from all people of goodwill for those who lost their lives."

In his homily on Palm Sunday, 2015, Father Miguel spoke of courage as well. He observed, that amid the glorious entry into Jerusalem, Jesus knew what was to happen only days away. Jesus knew that one of His beloved twelve would betray Him; that the one He had chosen to be the rock His Church would be built on would deny Him, not once or twice but three times; that the remaining apostles would essentially disappear in the hour of His need; that He would be physically abused in inhuman ways; that His Beloved Mother would witness the worst of His diabolical treatment; and that He would be unjustly nailed to the cross. Yet even though He was fully God, He was also fully human. In His humanity, Jesus knew the agony He would suffer, but He courageously walked toward His Passion, not away from it. Jesus courageously endured all the physical,

190

mental, emotional and spiritual agony that we would feel, simply because He loves us. Some theologians maintain that Jesus would have suffered even more than we would have, because He was perfectly human. Once again, *"I am the good shepherd. The good shepherd lays down his life for the sheep."*

I am reminded of the vivid conversations in the fall of 2014 about what was said, what was reportedly said and what might not have been said at the Extraordinary Synod of Bishops on the Family, convened by Pope Francis in Rome. The secular media had a field day speculating about how the Church is about to change it teachings on a variety of issues including gay marriage, reception of the sacraments by those who have divorced but have not gone through reconciliation with Church laws, etc. Even devout Catholics were buying into the hype. But Pope Francis made it quite clear from the outset of his Papacy that he encourages what he calls 'messy' dialogue and that while often quite uncomfortable, the messiness needs to happen if all sides of any issue are to be laid bare. Similarly, the pope is a strong believer in and has repeated often that he believes the clergy should take on the smell of their flock, and the only way to do that is be with them.

Two other sticky events have occurred recently that brought up additional delicate matters. In the spring of 2015, the Pope met with representatives of the U.S. Leadership Conference of Women Religious, the group of nuns Pope Benedict had appointed a panel of three bishops to overhaul. While full details are not yet available (at the time this was written), the essence of the agreement, arrived at two years earlier than expected, was that the nuns had gifts, the Church has gifts and both sides should work together to use those gifts for the greater good of the flock. Courage was exercised in both situations in dealing with conflict head on.

But as I read the Bull of Indiction for the upcoming Jubilee Year of Mercy to begin December 8, 2015, I could not help but do so in the context of the 2014 Synod and the Pope's meeting with the women religious. As I studied the bull and read the Catholic News Services' coverage (and I strongly believe that the Year of Mercy is at least as important as, if not more so, than the recently celebrated Year of Faith (2013)), Psalm 85:8 came to mind:

Show us, LORD, your mercy; grant us your salvation.

I could not help but wonder whether these multiple events were connected in some fundamental way – a way that might make me squirm – only time will tell. Might the Year of Mercy be the mechanism to offer forgiveness and welcome to many outside of or away from the church back into it? Might the realization of God's love for us be shown by His mercy on those who are at odds with the Church? Might we be seeing a precursor of changes about to be made in teachings of the Church that devout Catholics have held dear for their lifetimes? Might our Catholic brothers and sisters who have suffered through a divorce but have not realigned with the Church via the tribunal process be allowed once again to receive the sacraments? How about the welcoming of gays to a sacramental life? Mind you, I am not predicting any of these outcomes, necessarily in favor of them, and clearly I do not know whether they are even being seriously debated; however, should the Magisterium adopt such decisions, or any other that would challenge the orthodoxy that I have been comfortable with for decades, would I, would you, have the courage to obey – or would I dig in and resist? From deep within me, I hope and pray I would find the courage to obey.

I am reminded by my friend Dusty Staub that we need not only to have the courage to act, but the courage to see current realities, to be vulnerable, to love, to learn and grow, and to confront and be confronted. To Dusty's list I would add, "Lord, give me the courage to be your devoted servant, to fulfill my mission, no matter how difficult it might be for me to do so."

Is it necessary that we suffer physical injury, contract diseases unfairly, choose an occupation specifically dedicated to serving others, be falsely imprisoned, starved, or martyred to show courage in the face of danger or hardship? The answer is obviously "no." However, we are asked to courageously defend our faith, stay true to our faith, help others come to the faith, and serve others as Jesus taught us to serve others, praying for those who endure the most difficult and painful situations.

In the face of danger or discomfort, would I be willing to say, "I am Catholic" (or Christian), knowing that doing so would result in my torture, death or both?" Or would I be like Peter on the night Jesus was arrested (as I so often am) and deny Him. And if I personally find it difficult to accept a change, any change, in Church teachings by the Magisterium, will I have the courage to lean into His Grace and follow?

Reflection

Sustenance for Serving Graciously –
The Real-Presence Conversation

*Then he took the bread, said the blessing, broke it,
and gave it to them, saying, "This is my body, which
will be given for you; do this in memory of me."
(Luke 22:19)*

One of the most sacred fundamental teachings of the Catholic Church that differentiates us from all other Christian denominations is our belief in Transubstantiation. The Catholic Church teaches that during the Consecration of the Mass, the *substance* of the bread and wine is changed into the body, blood, soul and divinity of Christ Himself, the very essence of our belief in the Real Presence of Christ in the Eucharist. The words of consecration prayed by the priest (who through his ordination can trace his capacity to act in *Persona Christi* – in the Person of Christ – all the way back to the apostles) are the means through which this miracle takes place. While the appearance of wafer and wine remain the same, their actual substance is no longer the same. Only through the gift of faith does this mystery make any sense because the physical, chemical and biological evidence remains the same after the consecration. The center of all Christian worship until the Reformation was always the Eucharist, not the sermon, as it is for Protestants (Kreeft. 2008). For Catholics the focal point remains the Eucharist, thus it is never omitted from the Mass.

Today, the Catholic Church teaches the reality of both the Real Presence and Transubstantiation (although some Lutherans and some Anglicans hold similar beliefs). Interestingly, many of the early key players in the Protestant Reformation – for example, Martin Luther and Henry VIII – continued to believe in the Real Presence, even though they disagreed with other teachings of the Church. Not until Ulrich Zwingli, an ordained Catholic priest like Martin Luther, who led the Reformation in Switzerland, did any of the nonheretical Protestant denominations challenge the Real Presence. Over the centuries, however, following his lead, such belief by many denominations has dwindled away. John Calvin, too, rejected transubstantiation and the Real Presence even though he taught that we receive Christ in the Eucharist but only in the spiritual or subjective sense.

For Catholics, our belief in the Real Presence of Jesus Christ in the Eucharist raises the Sacrament of the Holy Eucharist above all the other sacraments. According to Peter Kreeft (2008), two of the most perfect and powerful means to becoming a saint are participating in Eucharistic adoration (prayer before the exposed presence of the Blessed Sacrament) and frequently receiving Holy Communion – not because these two actions are more liturgically correct than others, and not because they are psychologically useful, but because Jesus Christ, the saint-maker, is present in the Eucharist as He is nowhere else in the world. And wherever He is present, He is active. Even when He waits patiently in the Tabernacle, disguised under the appearance of a little wafer of bread, He is acting. Many believe the sacraments are ladders God built for man to rise to Him. They are, in fact, ladders, but rather for God to descend to us. By descending to us, God provides the sustenance we need to carry out His work – lovingly and graciously serving others. The old adage, "You are what you eat" rings very true here.

Christ has died, Christ is risen, Christ will come again. The risen Christ gives Himself to us in the Eucharist and is present in a very real way during each and every mass offered. Putting this into context, Christ's death and Resurrection are played out thousands of times daily in every corner of the globe. Mere words cannot emphasize the importance of believing this reality – the Holy Eucharist is the very source and summit of our Catholic faith. One of the highest order feast days of our liturgical year (a Solemnity) is dedicated to the Feast of Corpus Christi, the Feast of the Body and Blood of Christ, a glorious celebration of our belief in the Real Presence through Transubstantiation.

Our belief in the Real Presence is not based on some pious notion made up by Church leaders. Rather, the Eucharist *REALLY IS* the body and blood of Christ. Proof is taken directly from John 6:53-56, 60, and 66-69:

Jesus said to them, "Amen, amen, I say to you, unless you eat the flesh of the Son of Man and drink his blood, you do not have life within you. Whoever eats my flesh and drinks my blood has eternal life, and I will raise him on the last day. For my flesh is true food, and my blood is true drink. Whoever eats my flesh and drinks my blood remains in me and I in him.

Then many of his disciples who were listening said, "This saying is hard; who can accept it?"

As a result of this, many [of] his disciples returned to their former way of life and no longer accompanied him. Jesus then said to the Twelve, "Do you also want to leave?" Simon Peter answered him, "Master, to whom shall we go? You have the words of eternal life. We have come to believe and are convinced that you are the Holy One of God."

Further, in the Last Supper narrative appearing in all three of the synoptic Gospels (Matthew 26:26, Mark 14:22 and Luke 22:19), Jesus says:

"This IS my body…"

Jesus does not say, "this is sort of my body and blood"; or "this represents my body and blood"; or "it is up to you to decide if you think it might be my real body and blood." Jesus says very clearly, *"THIS IS MY BODY."* Faith allows us to believe what we cannot see and cannot prove scientifically. When we open our hearts and minds to the Holy Spirit, we are freely given the faith to believe. And when we receive the Holy Eucharist into our body, we are as close to Christ at that moment as we can get. We encounter, in the most profound way, the risen living Christ. Feeding on the Holy Eucharist is even more important to nourishing our souls than eating normal food is to nourishing our bodies. Our ability to serve others graciously can only be done enthusiastically when our spirit has been nourished with the living presence of Our Lord. Why? Because just as our physical bodies atrophy without eating regularly, the same thing happens to our souls when we do not feed them by receiving the Holy Eucharist, by praying or doing some other sort of spiritually nourishing activity regularly. Receiving Holy Communion frequently should be at the forefront of our minds and hearts.

Preparing spiritually and physically to receive Holy Communion should be done thoughtfully. In a similar way that Jewish tradition required ritual washing as part of their liturgies, our reception of the Holy Eucharist requires our soul to be clean. In short, we need to take a spiritual shower. As Catholics, we call such spiritual washing the Sacrament of Reconciliation. If we are guilty of serious sin, we are obliged to have those wrongs absolved through confession before receiving Holy Communion. We should prepare physically as well, washed and dressed appropriately to receive the Lord, particularly at Sunday Mass. Being dressed like we are going to the gym, most of the time, is inappropriate. To be sure there are occasions when it is not possible to attend mass in clean appropriate clothes, but those occasions should be the exception not the rule. How we present ourselves to receive Holy Communion speaks volumes about what we truly believe.

During the *Year of Faith* (November 2012 to October 2013) Pope Benedict XVI called for the entire faithful to renew and/or grow in the knowledge of our faith so we can fully participate in the new evangelization Saint John Paul II challenged us to be involved in. No matter if we are young, old, large or small; we have the responsibility to get ourselves to heaven. But each of us also has the obligation to help get others to heaven (to evangelize). If you are husband or wife, a parent, grandparent, you have the responsibility to teach those coming along behind you and help your spouse and children get to heaven. None of this is really new – Jesus actually asked each of us to evangelize while He was on earth. Matthew 28:16-20 is often referred to as The Great Commission:

The eleven disciples went to Galilee, to the mountain to which Jesus had ordered them. When they saw him, they worshiped, but they doubted. Then Jesus approached and said to them, "All power in heaven and on earth has been given to me. Go, therefore, and make disciples of all nations, baptizing them in the name of the Father, and of the Son, and of the Holy Spirit, teaching them to observe all that I have commanded you. And behold, I am with you always, until the end of the age."

In addition to directing us to evangelize, another important reality in this passage is perhaps the clearest expression about the Trinity found in sacred Scripture – Baptize them "In the name of the Father...Son...Holy Spirit." While these words may have been designated as the baptismal formula of the Church in Matthew's gospel, the words clearly designate the effect of baptism, specifically, the union of the one baptized with the Father, Son, and Holy Spirit.

In the Eucharist, Jesus does not literally bleed and die again – the sacrifice of the Cross was given "once and for all" and finished. It is not re-sacrificed rather re-offered in an unbloody manner. As such, we do not go back in history, rather history comes to us. But let there be no doubt, we do literally eat and drink His Body and Blood. He is really present, fully present, body, and blood, soul and divinity in both elements. We believe it is true because Jesus told us it is true. The Eucharist is the greatest gift we are ever given, and it is our gift through faith.

I received my First Holy Communion in first grade. No doubt early on, my teachers taught me a prayer of thanksgiving to say after receiving Holy Communion, but if they did, that prayer was lost decades ago. For most of my life I have said a prayer of thanksgiving after communion, but for years I have genuinely felt that my prayer was scattered, erratic or not sufficiently reverent or respectful. So I have been searching and yearning for a prayer that would be an appropriate response to the miraculous gift I have just been given. My friend, Deacon Jim Stone, suggested the *Anima Christi* (The Soul of Christ), the prayer of thanksgiving he says after communion. The prayer is simply beautiful. Many attribute the authorship of the prayer to St. Ignatius of Loyola; however, a nearly identical version of the prayer he used in his *Spiritual Exercises* can be found in prayer books written in the mid fourteenth century, more than a century and a half before Ignatius was born. Regardless, the prayer has been around for a very long time. Several different translations exist, but all convey the same beautiful message:

Soul of Christ, make me holy.
Body of Christ, save me.
Blood of Christ, fill me with love.
Water from Christ's side, wash me.
Passion of Christ, strengthen me.
Good Jesus, hear me.
Within your wounds, hide me.
Never let me be parted from you.
From the evil enemy, protect me.
At the hour of my death, call me
And tell me to come to you,
That with your saints I may praise you through all eternity. Amen

My wife and I both find this prayer to be a fitting way to thank Jesus for His coming into us through the Eucharist. At our parish, the prayer is near the back of our in-pew missalette, but if we find ourselves attending Mass at a church that does not have the prayer in their missalette, we have access to it via the mobile phone app *Laudate* (muted, of course!) and so it is always with us. How perfectly fitting to receive the *Body* and *Blood* of Christ in the Eucharist, then in thanksgiving pray the *Soul* of Christ reflecting on the *Divinity* of Christ.

Recently, my granddaughter was talking with me about some of the details of her upcoming First Holy Communion. As she spoke, I could not stop thinking about how she described this life-forming event. For many, the term "First Communion" is quite common. But her reference was clearly more specific than first communion. I quickly asked myself "How often do I really think about going to communion or receiving communion," rather than her far more descriptive and accurate "Holy Communion." Without knowing it, she metaphorically shook me back to a clearer awareness that the Eucharist is indeed "Holy." At the end of her First Holy Communion mass, the celebrant invited all the first communicants to wear their white dresses and suits to Sunday mass the following day, so that they could be recognized at whichever mass they attended. His purpose in doing so was to help remind the many of us who tend to slide into complacency to get ourselves back on track, attest to the holiness of the Eucharist, to openly declare the Real Presence of Christ in Holy Communion, and to return to the same level of devotion that we had when we received our First Holy Communion. Actually, my granddaughter, so special and so young, got me back on track much earlier, as she personally reminded me of the holiness of the Eucharist. My job now is to not forget the importance of her lesson over the next two years when her younger brother receives his First **Holy** Communion. Then I must continue to remember that important reality going forward.

The final Morning Prayer from the Liturgy of the Hours for the Feast of Corpus Christi beautifully sums up the linkage between our frequent reception of the Holy Eucharist and carrying out our baptismal obligation to graciously serve others:

Lord Jesus Christ, we worship you living among us in the sacrament of your body and blood. May we offer to our Father in heaven a solemn pledge of undivided love. May we offer to our brothers and sisters a life poured out in loving service of that kingdom where you live with the Father and the Holy Spirit, one God, for ever and ever.

Reflection

Prayer – Nourishing Our Relationship with God

~∞~

One of his disciples said to Him, "Lord teach us to pray." (Luke 11:1)

St. Therese of Lisieux was once asked her definition of prayer. Her reply was: "For me, prayer is a surge of the heart; it is a simple look turned toward heaven, it is a cry of recognition and of love, embracing both trial and joy." What a profound yet straightforward reply to a critical life question, offered by a young woman barely in her twenties. Prayer can be just as beautifully simple as the examples described by the Little Flower; yet, Part IV of *Catechism of the Catholic Church* devotes more that eighty pages to the subject of prayer, with extensive referencing on each page, creating a remarkable treasury of thoughts about, guidelines for, understanding of and insights into the meaning of prayer consolidating a myriad of volumes written about it.

Prayer has always been a part of my life. Some of my earliest memories include childhood nighttime prayers, family mealtime blessings, attending Mass every Sunday, and the multiple-times-a-day prayers that were part of attending a Catholic school from kindergarten through high school. Most of the prayers during the early part of my life were initiated and guided by my parents and teachers and usually consisted of the Our Father, Hail Mary, Glory Be, Apostles Creed and Act of Contrition. But eventually, the choice to pray, and how to pray, rested solely on my own shoulders. "To pray or not to pray, that is the question."

I would like to say that I took up the challenge of praying on my own, internalized the challenge, then developed healthy prayer habits – but I cannot. Unfortunately, I found the discipline to pray regularly was (is) at least as difficult, if not more so, as the discipline to exercise. If it takes effort and it must be done regularly, well.... And on the occasions I did choose to pray, often it was to do the *quid quo pro* kind of praying. You know, "Okay God, if you will do this, I will do that." "If you will get me through this senior English exam with at least a 'B,' I will attend an extra daily mass each week for a month!" I must admit to praying that way far too many times. And while prayers of petition with conditions are better than not praying at all, doesn't God deserve better? In fact, if for no other reason than I was anointed priest at baptism, I have the responsibility (as a priest) to pray, especially for the kingdom, the reality far beyond the boundary of ourselves.

St. John Damascene offered this classic definition of prayer: "Prayer is the raising of one's mind and heart to God or the requesting of good things from God." (*De Fide Orth. 3, 24*) I am paraphrasing from *The Catechism* (Paragraphs 2559-2561):

> When we pray, do we speak from the height of our pride and will, or "out of the depths" of a humble and contrite heart? Humility is the foundation of prayer. "Only when we pray as we ought," are we ready to receive freely the gift of prayer. "Man is a beggar before God."...Whether we realize it or not, prayer is the encounter of God's thirst with ours. God thirsts that we may thirst for him.
>
> Christian prayer is a covenant relationship between God and man in Christ. It is the action of God and of

man, springing forth from both the Holy Spirit and ourselves, wholly directed to the Father, in union with the human will of the Son of God made man.

Clearly prayer is about more than my needs; more than me asking for favors in desperation for myself or others; and more than just being thankful for good things that might have happened. Because prayer is the essence of the covenant relationship between me and my God – Father, Son and Holy Spirit – it must also include prayers of adoration and contrition. Prayer is the primary portal of communication that allows me to be open to God's plan for my life. John Henry Newman said this beautifully: "God has created me to do Him some definite service. He has committed some work to me which He has not committed to another. I have my mission."

Prayer is the necessary ingredient in the recipe for our spiritual and emotional health, or should I say, for my spiritual and emotional health. It is simply not possible for me to maintain a healthy relationship with my loving Lord, without an energetic, devoted discipline of interaction with Him.

Suffice it to say that as I got through high school and college, started my career, got married and started a family, I drifted into and out of good prayer habits, likely dictated by my personal needs, the jams I was in, or the needs of my family and my job. After significant reflection, I was reminded of several situations over the years that have critically influenced the formation of my personal prayer life and the prayer life I have with my wife. I would like to share a few of them with you. Under no circumstance should my remarks here suggest in any way that I have figured all this out – actually quite the contrary.

My job required us to move frequently during the first dozen years of our marriage. One such transfer sent us to

Augusta, Maine, for my first management assignment. The most senior fellow in my new office had been passed over twice for my job. I was just thirty-two years old and he had been with the agency thirty-three years. He worked hard at getting under my skin, but I was determined he would never know he succeeded. One day my colleague came to my office in tears with the news his wife had been diagnosed with cancer. I sat beside him for a while, and then with my hand on his shoulder, told him we would be praying for his wife and family. From that moment, our relationship changed. Never again did I split wood mumbling his name as I swung the ax. Until that day with Glenn, I had never mentioned prayer, religion or God at work, but I learned the immense value in allowing my total self to be revealed, even on the job. The mere promise of prayer for another can be remarkably enriching. But we did pray for Glenn's family as we promised and for many others over the years.

In spite of what some think, God always answers our prayers, but His answers are in His time and for our ultimate good rather in our time and what we want. God does not ignore us. While Laurel and I were still in Maine, we discovered the importance of a sustained trusting prayer relationship. We were already blessed with two beautiful, healthy children – and Laurel was pregnant with our third. As we had done both times before, we prayed for a healthy baby. The pregnancy seemed normal until about the halfway point when some tests began to concern the doctors, even though Laurel appeared to be doing fine. But as her delivery date approached, she, too, began to feel something might be wrong. On the morning of May 16, 1980, we went to the hospital. Our baby was alive but struggling in the labor room so an emergency C-section was done. Very early in the procedure, however, our baby's heart stopped, and even the small army of doctors attending could do nothing. With all of our family's hopes for our new baby, and after a full-term pregnancy, Thomas became our family's first angel. We were devastated. Why had God allowed our baby to die? Why were our prayers for a healthy baby unanswered? After many tears, much sorrow, and hours of reflection, we began to realize that God had in fact answered our prayers. We had prayed for a healthy baby, but the baby did not develop normally. Had he been born alive, he would likely have suffered much and likely not survived for more than a few hours, days, or weeks. His loss after having him alive in our arms would have been even more difficult than his death at birth. While we suffered significant pain, we were spared a more difficult outcome.

Not long after starting my next assignment, in Atlanta, in the spring of 1981, I had a very difficult meeting with the head of a key state funding agency. A couple of years before, with the help from some of his staff, our office supervised their entry of data into an important data base, only to find out later, the data were unreliable – a serious situation for an agency priding itself on quality data and analysis. As I drove downtown from Doraville, I prayed for guidance on how to deal with the situation. No inspiration came. I rode the elevator to the fourth floor – still nothing. My colleague's greeting was chilly, but as I began to speak, I seemed to have no control over of the words coming out of my mouth. As I responded and asked questions, Bill warmed up. In less than an hour, we devised a strategy to fix the problem, agreed to share the cost, and developed metrics to track progress. What a miraculous intervention. How could I possibly forget the way the Lord answered my prayers.

Several years later I learned a valuable lesson about how our prayers are often answered through others. My wife and I were attending a scripture study class led by a dear friend. We had finished the "Acts of the Apostles" a week early, but everyone decided to meet for the last class anyway. That Friday, I was told by one of our research managers that the funding he had promised would not be coming. I was livid – maybe worse. How dare he? My secretary made a reservation for me for a late Sunday night flight to DC. I made an appointment to see the guy's boss. I was loaded for bear, my rage only marginally contained. That weekend, I was fit to be tied, but we went to our scripture class in spite of my foul mood. For our discussion that day, our friend Bob had "randomly" chosen, James 1:19-20:

Keep this in mind, dear brothers. Let every man be quick to hear, slow to speak, slow to anger, for a man's anger does not fulfill God's justice.

Hearing that passage hit me like a lightning bolt – the Lord had spoken directly to my pain through Holy Scripture. My chin dropped and my face went pale. Bob asked "Are you okay?" Barely able to talk, I told the class what had happened Friday and my plans for Monday. But just a few seconds earlier, the revealed word of God had changed most of that – my prayers had been answered in a way I had never expected. I did go to DC that night, but the rest played out quite differently than originally planned. The first person I ran into Monday was the number two guy in our agency, with whom I had a great relationship. He asked what brought me to town, so I calmly explained. He listened, then called the program manager in and asked his side of the story. Bottom line, our funding was restored and was continued to the planned end of the project. During the meeting, I was totally silent. Had I done what I set out to do, and not followed the advice from James, the outcome would surely have been a disaster. Whenever I seem to need it most, the Lord gets my attention with a gentle swat!

One of shortest, most frequently prayed prayers is often not even recognized as prayer, even by Catholics. "In the name of the Father, and of the Son and of the Holy Spirit.

Amen." Yes, the Sign of the Cross is a prayer, a profoundly beautiful prayer affirming our deep belief in the Blessed Trinity. We normally pray those words with the physical signing of ourselves visually declaring the importance of Christ dying on the cross for us. Typically, we pray the Sign of the Cross often, both before and after most other prayers. Yet how often do we go through the motions or slur the words, mostly unconscious of the importance of what we are praying and doing and why we are doing it? It's what we Catholics do, so I do it, but fail to really "pray" the prayer.

Sadly, we allow ourselves to drift into bad habits, most of the time not realizing we are doing so – even when praying the Sign of the Cross. I became aware of such a bad habit I had slipped into about ten years ago when Laurel and I were in Charleston visiting our son, David, and his fiancée, Patti, on the occasion of her Confirmation, with Dave as her sponsor. We were seated several rows behind the confirmants and their sponsors. At the outset of Mass, I must admit I had my eyes focused on the young couple. As the bishop began Mass with the Sign of the Cross, I could not help but notice the deep reverence with which Patti responded. I was deeply touched. Through the years, I had allowed myself to get sloppy in praying this short, beautiful acclimation, but through the tears, watching Patti do so slowly, deliberately and reverently I became aware of the profound lesson she unknowingly taught me. My contact lenses were out of control for a while. Throughout the decade since that moment, I have tried hard to always pray the Sign of the Cross with the devotion the Trinity deserves. Thank you, Patti, for reminding me just how important that is.

About a month before our younger grandson was born, our daughter Amy's physician discovered that our grandson had a condition that would require surgery very soon after he was born. Needless to say, such news landed hard on us. Even though our daily prayers throughout her pregnancy had been for a healthy baby and easy delivery, the news jolted us into realizing we needed to be more aggressive in our prayers. So, we jointly decided to add praying the Rosary daily. Nicholas was born without complication, and at 6 weeks underwent the surgery needed to repair the problem. After only about 2½ months of praying the rosary, and having our prayers answered so remarkably, we decided to continue including that beautiful prayer. Seven plus years later, the rosary is an entrenched part of our daily routine and continues to be a blessing for us.

Three years ago, Laurel was diagnosed with breast cancer, and even though there was a family history of the disease, the news about her condition came as a shock. The "C" word nearly always sends shock waves of fear, concern and anxiety, not only through the patient but also through the patient's family and friends. We decided that we would face the challenge head-on together and do everything we could to get her healed. We knew that prayer must be the foundation upon which we would make decisions about her treatment and guide her recovery. So we chose to be open with everyone we know about what was going on in our lives, asking each of them to pray for her. The response was extraordinary. Not only did our family and friends join the journey with us, within a very short time we became aware that our network of prayer warriors had grown exponentially, including many people we did not even know – friends-of-friends, etc. As we went to the requisite doctors' appointments, preliminary testing, and surgery scheduling, both of us felt a profound sense of calm – the direct result of our prayer-support family. As the day of surgery approached our family gathered to support us, and on the day of surgery the sense of peace both Laurel and I felt with family around us and the prayer warriors at work was remarkable, frankly indescribable. My thoughts continually replayed the rhetorical question, "How could anyone face such a trying time without prayer?" Even after her surgeries, the prayers continued to flood us, to the point that I began responding to the "How is she doing?" question with "the tidal wave of prayer support we have felt has been overwhelming." Our post surgery visits with the medical and radiation oncologists as well as with her surgeon and plastic surgeon all yielded the good news, all margins were clean, no need for chemotherapy, no need for radiation, no need for any follow-on medication. The miracle so many had prayed for was granted her. Thankfully, she is back to normal on all fronts, is strong, vibrant and full of energy living life as she has always done. Thank you, Jesus, for her treatment and full recovery. Thank you, Jesus, for the support of family and friends. Thank you, Jesus, for the prayer support of not just family and friends, but also for the many who prayed for her that even now remain unknown to us. What more wonderful gift can you give anyone than to pray for them in their time of need?

Laurel and I have prayed together nearly daily, for more than twenty-five years, but praying together was not always part of our life. Once we decided to start we found it quite awkward, so we started slowly with simple prayers and the daily scripture readings from the Mass and a meditation on those readings. Over time, as we became more and more comfortable with this new part of our life together, we developed prayer habits that now seem quite natural and comfortable.

After about ten years of our praying together, my job required me to be out of town most week days, every week. While it took us a while to figure out what was negatively impacting our relationship during those very short weekends at home, we finally realized our daily prayer time had taken a back seat to the 700 miles separating us. So for the rest of the time I was gone so much, we simply had a "prayer date" on the phone each morning at 7:00 a.m. What a difference that made. And, what a blessing praying together daily continues to be for us.

One of the most sweeping, relatively new additions to our daily devotions began early in 2013, following a class taught by our dear friend Deacon Jim Stone. Having never really been exposed to The Divine Office (sometimes called The Breviary or Liturgy of the Hours) except knowing that all priests, religious, and ordained deacons are required to pray these prayers daily, we discovered the remarkable beauty of praying the Psalms. The psalm and canticle selections for each day, along with Old and New Testament readings and other prayers added a depth and enrichment we were looking for in our devotions. Knowing that those same prayers are being said continuously around the globe every day also provides us a genuine sense of belonging to the universality of the Church. The discipline of committing to pray, even just the "Morning Prayers" part of the Liturgy, has yielded remarkable joy, comfort and understanding to our daily life. Because the Divine Office is available online and accessible through our smart phones, we have no excuse for missing a day!

And the most recent addition to our prayers together is a prayer that had previously been mostly unknown to us, the Divine Mercy Chaplet. The Chaplet is simple to pray, takes very little time to complete, and provides a beautiful opportunity to pray for very special intentions. Because we seem to always have such special intentions to pray for, the Divine Mercy Chaplet is now a part of our prayers for others.

It would be nice to be able to say I am doing all I need to do to nourish my relationship with my loving Lord – but I cannot. I sometimes postpone praying now with the intent of praying later, then the day ends I have not done so. My prayers are often interrupted with distractions. Far too often I am willing to rush through my routine because I have convinced myself that time is short – but what could be more important? While reasonably disciplined about praying with Laurel, I am not so dedicated to private prayers. And while prayers of petition and thanksgiving seem to come pretty easy, other types of prayer are much harder. And I still do not spend sufficient time in adoration.

Clearly I am still very much a work in progress, hopefully moving forward rather than slipping backward. How about you?

Reflection

XXIV

Baptism – The Anointing to Evangelize

*It happened in those days that Jesus came from
Nazareth of Galilee and was baptized in the Jordan
by John. (Mark 1:9)*

As Catholic Christians, we believe our baptism influences
and gives meaning to our personal sharing in Christ's
incarnation, His earthly ministry, and His suffering, death
and resurrection for the expiation of our sins. But our baptism
also has significant implications about the responsibilities we
each share for spreading the word of God and all of what that
means in the context of the new evangelization into which
we are called. Equally important, our baptism sheds a bright
light onto what God has planned for us, the mission of our
lives, the part we play in His far grander plan for humanity,
and how we must be dedicated to serving others.

An important feast day celebrated by the Catholic Church
is the feast of the Baptism of Jesus. In the gospel reading
for the feast, Mark 1:7-11, John the Baptist announces the
coming of Jesus:

*And this is what he proclaimed: "One mightier than
I is coming after me. I am not worthy to stoop and
loosen the thongs of his sandals. I have baptized
you with water; he will baptize you with the Holy
Spirit." It happened in those days that Jesus came
from Nazareth of Galilee and was baptized in the*

*Jordan by John. On coming up out of the water he
saw the heavens being torn open and the Spirit, like
a dove, descending upon him. And a voice came from
the heavens, "You are my beloved Son; with you I am
well pleased."*

A beautiful foretelling of our Baptism in Christ was provided
by Ezekiel, the first prophet called to prophesy outside the
Holy Land, while the Israelites were still in exile in Babylon
about six centuries before the birth of Jesus. Following the
destruction of Jerusalem by Nebuchadnezzar, Ezekiel's
prophecies were characterized by the promise of salvation
in a new covenant and the conditions required to obtain it
(Ezekiel 36:25-28):

*I will sprinkle clean water over you to make you clean;
from all your impurities and from all your idols I will
cleanse you. I will give you a new heart, and a new
spirit I will put within you. I will remove the heart of
stone from your flesh and give you a heart of flesh. I
will put my spirit within you so that you walk in my
statutes, observe my ordinances, and keep them. You
will live in the land I gave to your ancestors; you will
be my people, and I will be your God.*

I was blessed to hear a wonderful homily preached by
Father Miguel on the feast of the Baptism of Jesus, based
on this reading from Saint Mark's gospel. The initial idea he
presented was that Jesus did not need to be baptized, for two
reasons. First, the purpose of baptism for us is to remove the
stain of original sin and Jesus clearly did not have original
sin because, even though He was fully human, He was also
fully divine. The second reason is that baptism "grafts" us
into or onto the Mystical Body of Christ and Jesus had no
need to do that either because He IS Christ. So why did Jesus
humble Himself and invite John to baptize Him in precisely

216

the same way that he, John, baptized everyone else? I believe that this beautiful act of humility was Jesus' way of inviting us, by way of His own personal example, into an intimate, loving relationship with Him, similar to the relationship that He has with His Father. In so doing we are drawn into a communion of sharing in the fruits of His life, death and resurrection. Remember, Jesus did not "have" to do that – but He did.

Hebrews 4:14-16 says:

Since we have a great high priest who has passed through the heavens, Jesus, the Son of God, let us hold fast to our confession. For we do not have a high priest who is unable to sympathize with our weaknesses, but one who has similarly been tested in every way, yet without sin. So let us confidently approach the throne of grace to receive mercy and to find grace for timely help.

During his homily, Father Miguel talked about the visual image of our baptism grafting us to Christ's Mystical Body – an image that is particularly meaningful to me. I "get" the issue of "grafting." About ten or so years ago, in an accident in my workshop, I managed to partially amputate a finger on my right hand – more specifically I cut a quarter of an inch off the middle digit. As I exited the workshop to clean the wound, I realized that from what I could see (or should I say, not see) there likely was a part of me left on the saw table. In fact, I was able to find an eighth of an inch of my finger tip lying there. A hand surgeon was able to repair the fleshy part of my finger without a great deal of trouble, but the wound was sufficiently severe that part of my finger nail was also removed. As part of the surgery, the doctor grafted the salvaged nail-bed tissue (taken from the remnant of me) back onto my finger. He advised me that the graft may or may not take. As luck would have it, the graft did take, so my damaged digit is whole (albeit shorter), fully useful, and with full feeling. My point in relating this story is that the graft done on my finger attached a damaged part of me back onto me and that graft is fully part of me, just like it was before the accident. When our baptism grafts us onto the Mystical Body of Christ, we become a very real part of Christ – not an appendage, not something added, not a patch. We become part of His Body, just like the nail bed tissue on my finger is again fully a part of me, a functioning part of my finger and hand that will remain that way – unless, of course there is another traumatic incident! Similarly, we remain part of the Mystical Body of Christ unless we choose to separate ourselves from the love of God by a traumatic incident – when we consciously choose to deny Him.

After meditating on this issue for some time, it occurred to me that some of the remarkable passages in Chapter 6 of St. John's gospel might also shed light on still another possible reason why Jesus asked John to baptize Him. In John 6:35 Jesus said:

> **"I am the bread of life;** *whoever comes to me will never hunger, and whoever believes in me will never thirst."*

A few verses later, Jesus made one of the most profound declarations in all of Scripture, the truth of which, sadly, is denied even by many Catholics. John 6:51, 53-58. Jesus said:

> *"I am the living bread that came down from heaven; whoever eats this bread will live forever; and the bread that I will give is my flesh for the life of the world…." Jesus said to them, "Amen, amen, I say to you, unless you eat the flesh of the Son of Man and drink his blood, you do not have life within you. Whoever eats my flesh and drinks my blood has*

218

*eternal life, and I will raise him on the last day. For
my flesh is true food, and my blood is true drink.
Whoever eats my flesh and drinks my blood remains
in me and I in him. Just as the living Father sent me
and I have life because of the Father, so also the one
who feeds on me will have life because of me. This is
the bread that came down from heaven. Unlike your
ancestors who ate and still died, whoever eats this
bread will live forever."*

Many of His disciples said that hearing such words was
"hard, who could accept it?" And many walked away. Even
the apostles had a difficult time, to the point that Jesus asked
them if they too wanted to leave. Peter, speaking for the
others said (John 6:68):

*"Master, to whom shall we go? You have the words
of eternal life."*

The point of all this is that we must eat Jesus' flesh to
have life. We must eat the bread of life to survive eternity.
Luke 13:21 says that the kingdom of God

*...is like **yeast** that a woman took and mixed [in] with
three measures of wheat flour until the whole batch
of dough was leavened.*

Even though the bread of the Eucharist as we receive
it is usually unleavened, symbolically yeast is a primary
ingredient of the bread we eat. Time after time throughout
the New Testament we find references to the "Bread of Life,"
to yeast, the eternal food and images of what the kingdom
of God is like. When Jesus waded into the Jordan, is it not
possible that He was providing the leavening for the bread
of life we must eat to live? By His loving example, might
His presence in the river, humbling Himself to be baptized
by someone "not worthy to loosen his sandals," leavened

the entirety of human kind? Our baptism admits us into an intimate relationship with Him. Our baptism opens the door to sharing eternity with our loving Father. Our baptism ordains us as missionaries sharing in the responsibility of the new evangelization to spread His Good News.

The challenge of evangelization is not a choice that we can just accept if we feel like it, maybe flipping a coin with a heads or tails outcome. Rather, being a missionary, evangelizing to those around us and possibly to those far away, is what it means to be appointed priest. As a reminder, near the end of the Catholic Rite of Baptism the celebrant says these words, "He now anoints you with the chrism of salvation. As Christ was anointed Priest, Prophet, and King, so may you live always as a member of His body, sharing in the everlasting life." We are anointed Priest. We are made members of His body and as such we share in the responsibilities of being a member of His body. Our reward for being "good and faithful servants" or priests, sharing the gospel with others, is that we are assured we will share the joy of everlasting life with Father, Son and Holy Spirit.

Pope Francis' recent Apostolic Exhortation entitled, *Evangelii Gaudium,* or, *The Joy of the Gospel,* deals extensively with the importance of preaching the gospel. He uses very clear language directed to the clergy about their responsibility for preparing and preaching quality homilies, and all of that is as it should be and frankly what I expected he would teach. But Pope Francis is quite clear about the massive responsibilities that we, the laity, have for spreading the gospel, as well as constantly being in missionary mode, and ever vigilant for opportunities to evangelize. St. Francis is attributed with saying we have the responsibility of preaching the gospel always and when necessary use words.

The Pope's message closely parallels St. Francis's call to action. Specifically, referring to the Great Commission (Matthew 28:16-20), Francis says:

In virtue of their baptism, all members of the People of God have become missionary disciples. All the baptized, whatever their position in the Church or their level of instruction in the faith, are agents of evangelization...The new evangelization calls for personal involvement on the part of each of the baptized...Every Christian is a missionary to the extent that he or she has encountered the love of God in Christ Jesus.

Pope Francis lovingly reminds us that even in John 1:41:

The Samaritan woman became a missionary immediately after speaking with Jesus and many Samaritans came to believe in him "because of the woman's testimony."

Almost in the same breath he used to tell of Jesus' baptism in Chapter 1, Saint Mark related the calling of the first disciples and the first missionary trip to Capernaum where (Mark 1:21-22):

...on the Sabbath he entered the synagogue and taught. The people were astonished at his teaching, for he taught them as one having authority and not as the scribes.

A beautiful meditation on this verse from *The Word Among Us* says that we normally

think about the word 'authority' as meaning the right and ability to enforce rules. But when Jesus speaks with authority He is speaking about the things He wants to create and build in us. Consider this – by virtue of your baptism, Jesus says...

You are Safe – *I give you eternal life and no one can take you out of my hand. (John 10:28)*

You are Known Intimately – *Before you were born, my eyes gazed on your unformed substance. I know you inside and out, exactly how you are made. (Psalm 139:12-16)*

You are Chosen – *I chose you before the foundation of the world to be with me forever. (Ephesians 1:4)*

You are Treasured – *Even if a mother should forget her child, I will never forget you. (Isaiah 49:15)*

You are Empowered – *You can do all things, for I will strengthen you and give you the wisdom and power you need to do what I call you to do. (Philippians 4:13)*

All these statements are true about each of us. Let Jesus speak these words, in all His authority to us today. Let these words shape the way we relate to the people around us, too. For the more we know about how important we are to the Father, the more we will see how important everyone else is – and the more we will begin to treasure them.

Quoting St. Thomas Aquinas...*agere sequitur esse*... "I act according to who I am" (i.e. I act according to what I believe.) Who are you (am I)? What do you (I) believe? Answers to these questions profoundly influence everything we do – every day!

Epilogue

The Power of Living with Aggressive Humility

⸺∞⸺

As God's chosen ones, holy and beloved, clothe yourselves with compassion, kindness, humility, meekness, and patience. (Colossians 3:12)

One of my most significant lifelong personal struggles is that of overcoming pride – the unhealthy kind of pride that leads one to believe he is more important, that his ideas are better, that he is more deserving of the promotion, that his counsel is wiser, that his needs and aspirations are more important than those around him. Such pride leads us to treat others with disrespect, to climb over colleagues who get in our way, to be unwilling to share what we know with others, and to smother the imagination and enthusiasm of others so we can be the brightest star.

Prideful behavior blocks the path of humility that God asks us to tread, the same path that is required of us as servants, as servant leaders. Such conduct as being unwilling to admit mistakes or the tendency to judge others keeps us from becoming the servants, the persons that God created us to be. But let's be honest, finding fault in the words and actions of others is always easier than making courageous admissions of our own shortcomings. If only I would more frequently recall Jesus' admonition: remove the log from your own eye before removing the speck from your brother's eye.

Dorothy Sayer, in her highly acclaimed book, *Creed or Chaos?*, in a chapter entitled, "The Other Six Deadly Sins" states:

> But the head and origin of all sin is the basic sin of *Superbia* or Pride. In one way there is so much to say about Pride that one might speak of it for a week and not have done. Yet in another way, all there is to be said about it can be said in a single sentence. It is the sin of trying to be as God. It is the sin which proclaims that Man can produce out of his own wits and his own impulses and his own imagination the standards by which he lives: that Man is fitted to be his own judge. It is Pride which turns man's virtues into deadly sins, by causing each self-sufficient virtue to issue in its own opposite, and as a grotesque and horrible travesty of itself. The name under which Pride walks the world at this moment is the *Perfectibility of Man*, or the *Doctrine of Progress*; and its specialty is the making of blueprints for Utopia and establishing the Kingdom of Man on earth.

> For the devilish strategy of Pride is that it attacks us, not on our weak points, but on our strong. It is pre-eminently the sin of the noble mind – that *curruptio optimi* ("corruption of the best") which works more evil in the world than all the deliberate vices. Because we do not recognize pride when we see it, we stand aghast to see the havoc wrought by the triumphs of human idealism. We meant so well, we thought we were succeeding, and look what has come of our efforts! There is a proverb that says that the way to Hell is paved with good intentions. We usually take it as referring to intentions that have been weakly abandoned; but it has a deeper and much

subtler meaning. For that road is paved with good intentions strongly and obstinately pursued, until they have become self-sufficing ends in themselves and deified...

The Greeks feared above all things the state of mind they called *hubris* – the inflated spirits that come with too much success. Overweening in men called forth, they thought, the envy of the gods. Their theology may seem to us a little unworthy, but with the phenomenon itself and its effects they were only too well acquainted. Christianity, with a more rational theology, traces *hubris* back to the root sin of Pride, which places man instead of God at the center of gravity and so throws the whole structure of things into ruin called Judgment.

Sayer concludes:

Man cannot make himself happy by serving himself – not even when he calls self-service the service of the community; for "the community" in that context is only an extension of his own ego...It is of the essence of Pride to suppose that we can do without God.

"Pridefulness" plays out in many ways. For example, most of us like to be recognized for things we do, but some of us want to be praised constantly. And a few of us are compelled to look for admiration from others to boost the very sense of who we are. But if we hope to grow in humility, we must strip ourselves of such pride because pride is all about looking inward, whereas humility lovingly looks outward. I heard a wonderful expression recently that reveals why so many of us have such a hard time being humble. "I may not be much, but I'm all I think about."

The virtue of humility is defined in the *Catholic Encyclopedia* as, "A quality by which a person, considering his own defects, has a lowly opinion of himself and willingly submits himself to God and to others for God's sake." St. Bernard of Clairveaux, a twelfth century intellectual giant, defined humility as, "A virtue by which a man knowing himself as he truly is, abases himself." Both of these definitions correspond with that given by St. Thomas Aquinas: "The virtue of humility consists in keeping oneself within one's own bounds, not reaching out to things above one, but submitting to one's superior."

So, humility is based on the truth – the truth about God, the truth about the talents that God has given us, the honest truth about our shortcomings. Seems simple enough doesn't it? But there are significant barriers between us and the truth, including pride, vanity, arrogance and self-righteousness. All of a sudden, the diversions that keep us from being humble are a formidable minefield. As we climb our ladders of success, we often stray into this minefield with no idea we are there. When this happens, our ability to be role models for those around us suffers in direct proportion to how deeply we are mired in the minefield.

Thomas Williams in his book, *Spiritual Progress*, says:

Humility is the virtue that sifts through the many paradoxes of human existence in search of the truth. It peels off the layers of vanity and self-deception to reveal us to ourselves, as we really are. And it does so not by comparing us to other people to see how we stack up in the rogue's gallery of humanity but by placing us before the throne of God.

He goes on to say:

The truly humble person sees himself as he really is, since he sees himself as God sees him.

With this explanation, Williams provides a very similar description of the connection between humility and truth as C. S. Lewis did in his heavily acclaimed *Screwtape Letters.*

Truly humble living is about graciously serving others. As Catholic Christians we are chosen to be examples of such behavior. In 1849, Blessed John Henry Newman beautifully wrote, in *Discourses Addressed to Mixed Congregations*:

Everyone who breathes, high and low, educated and ignorant, young and old, man and woman, has a mission, has a work. We are not sent into this world for nothing; we are not born at random; we are not here, that we may go to bed at night, and get up in the morning, toil for our bread, eat and drink, laugh and joke, sin when we have a mind, and reform when we are tired of sinning, rear a family and die. God sees every one of us; He creates every soul...for a purpose. He needs, He deigns to need, every one of us. He has an end for each of us; we are all equal in His sight, and we are placed in our different ranks and stations, not to get what we can out of them for ourselves, but to labor in them for Him. As Christ has His work, we too have ours; as He rejoiced to do His work, we must rejoice in ours also.

The concept of being a good role model defines meaningful leadership. We must be about serving, not being served.

In several other reflections in this volume, I have shared my emerging thoughts on humility; however, my understanding of humility evolved to a new level after hearing a homily preached by Father John Anthony while on a mission trip to Honduras several years ago. The title of his sermon was "Aggressive Humility." I was startled to have the meaning of humility suddenly take on new dimensions when combined with aggressive. In *Some Practical Lessons in Leadership* (2010), I defined "aggressive humility" as the "passionate, unconditional devotion to the loving service of others," urging myself and others to embrace the power of leading (... or living) with aggressive humility. When we are dedicated to the *agape* or unconditional love of each person around us, we live selflessly, giving to others the best of what God gives to us. The epistle of James 2:14-17, 20-22, and 26 declares clearly:

> *What good is it, my brothers, if someone says he has faith but does not have works? Can that faith save him? If a brother or sister has nothing to wear and has no food for the day, and one of you says to them, "Go in peace, keep warm, and eat well," but you do not give them the necessities of the body, what good is it? So also faith of itself, if it does not have works, is dead...Do you want proof, you ignoramus, that faith without works is useless? Was not Abraham our father justified by works when he offered his son Isaac upon the altar? You see that faith was active along with his works, and faith was completed by the works... For just as a body without a spirit is dead, so also faith without works is dead.*

The faith that James speaks of here is the faith that lives out in the form of doing for others, not because we expect something in return but rather the opposite. That unconditional giving is driven by an aggressively humble spirit that treats everyone as the special child of God they are regardless of what they might say or do to us. As trite as it may sound, unconditional is just that – unconditional.

I find the challenge of being passionately dedicated to the loving service of others to be extremely difficult, not to mention being physically and emotionally exhausting. After a great deal of prayer and reflection, however, I must admit the fatigue is not really caused by the person I need to serve, rather, it is triggered by the person I see when I look into the mirror. Those not-so-easy-to-get-along-with or those not-so-pleasant-to-be-around stir me to be judgmental, arrogant, and patronizing (I could go on), forms of pride that are most unbecoming of a loving Catholic Christian. Chinks in my spiritual armor are readily visible to almost everyone except me. Lovingly serving others who are unpleasant or hard to get along with, or helping those who do not seem to have any interest in helping themselves simply drains energy. But what option is there? I could cite a number of possible (but worthless) options, but none makes any real sense. The answer to this question boils down to just one thing – Did Jesus give His life for me, or not? Clearly He died to atone for my sins and the sins of others. So, if He put no conditions on His gift to me, can I put conditions on others? While intellectually and spiritually I know I must follow Jesus' lead, doing so is very difficult at certain times and with certain people. The only way I can move forward in the way I live out being an anointed priest or servant is to constantly work hard to follow His lead, and when I come up short, when I stumble and fall (and I do that far too often), get up and try again.

There are a number of examples of passionate devotion to the unconditional service of others from which we can learn. For Christians the most obvious example is Jesus' death on the cross – for our sins. As Christians, we believe that He suffered and died for us. How coincidental that the word we use to describe the humiliation and suffering Jesus bore for us is *passion*. He could have easily by-passed the passion, He could have by-passed His crucifixion and death, but instead He passionately gave Himself for us and for our eternal salvation.

More recently, we can look to Blessed Mother Teresa of Calcutta. She was passionate and she was devoted to caring for the poorest of the poor. Even the most hardened cynic would have to admit that Mother Teresa was aggressively humble in her passionate devotion to caring for the needs of those forgotten in the gutters of Calcutta and other parts of the world.

For many, Pope Francis I is a very real, living example of an aggressively humble servant, meeting those he shepherds in the streets, on city buses, in hospitals, in orphanages. When he was archbishop of Buenos Aires, Jorge Maria Bergoglio frequently instructed his priests they should meet their flock where they live (like he did), to smell like their flock. Since the outset of his papacy his actions have been consistent with those instructions and have brought a new vision of what living humbly should be about.

These examples are merely the tip of the iceberg. We have a rich history of selfless people who have gone before us and others who may still be living with us today. But the real challenge for us as Christians is this – what can we personally do to be aggressively humble? To jump-start our understanding of what it means to be humble, imagine what it might be like to have lost everything. In Atlanta, Georgia, where I live, there are tens of thousands of people who have lost everything, or never had anything, who live on the streets, in stairways, under bridges, etc. As an eye-opener, imagine what it would be like to have so little that the only warm place you could find to sleep is in the corner of a public rest room. What would it be like to offer your morning or evening prayers with little to no hope in sight? With all semblances of pride wiped away, humility is what is left. You may know that the word *humility* is from the Latin root word *humus* meaning ground or soil. We humans are from the earth. The closer we are to the ground metaphorically, the closer we come to being humble.

So, here are a few suggestions for living with aggressive humility:

- Treat everyone you encounter with the same dignity and respect you would your dearest friend.
- When you have a disagreement with someone, even if you are only a tenth of one percent at fault, be first to apologize. Doing so accelerates reconciliation and provides an example to others.
- Be quick to recognize and give credit to God for your talents, successes, and gifts. Without those gifts nothing we would do would be possible anyway, so be truthful.
- Avoid being kind and generous just so others might have a higher opinion of us. Jesus admonished the right hand should not be aware of what the left hand is doing. Look for nothing in return.
- Pray the Litany of Humility regularly to remind yourself of the many blind spots that lead to pride. Remember, each incantation in the litany represents a form of humiliation that Jesus suffered while He was on earth – and we are subject to them as well.
- Dedicate time, energy and prayer to thinking more about the needs of others and less about your own needs – doing so is spiritually and psychologically healthy.
- Think about yourself less rather than thinking less of yourself. Recognizing the needs of others and taking action is easier when your ego is not in the way.
- No matter who you are with, make a point to be 100 percent present to them. As simple as this might sound, being fully present is really quite difficult because you must stop thinking of yourself!
- If you must take disciplinary action, whether as a parent or as a manager, be hard on the actions, soft on the other's dignity.
- Praise others selflessly and accept feedback courageously and graciously.

231

- When things go right share the credit. When things go wrong, accept responsibility and work hard to set things right.
- Keep the needs of others in the forefront of your thinking. I recently told my son I would pray for him as he faced a difficult conversation with a colleague the next day. He thanked me and accepted the offer. Then he asked that I pray for his colleague, too – such a small request, but what a huge indicator of an aggressively humble spirit. He taught me much through his request.

In spite of much study, prayer and contemplation on the topic, my understanding and practice of aggressive humility is unfortunately still in its infancy. Even so, I am fully convinced that aggressive humility is what God requires of me as a Christian. I am also convinced that I must practice aggressive humility in all aspects of my life if I have any hope of fulfilling the mission that God has created uniquely for me. As someone striving to do the right thing in all situations, but one who often makes mistakes, I still have a long way to grow.

So here is the difficult challenge: Do you have the courage to look truthfully at yourself, your actions, your thoughts and feelings? Do you have the courage to live all parts of your life with aggressive humility, serving those around you with generosity? If not, there is no time like the present to begin or begin again to muster that courage. If so, you might very well be on the way to fulfilling the special role that only you can fill, being the special link in a chain, a bond of connection between persons. Look around, watch, listen, observe – learn. "He did not create you for naught." But if along the way you become frightened or discouraged, I encourage you to reflect on the concluding words of Blessed John Henry Cardinal Newman's "Meditation on Christian Doctrine" (1848):

O Ruler of Israel...I give myself to Thee. I trust Thee wholly. Thou are wiser than I – more loving to me than I myself. Deign to fulfill Thy high purposes in me whatever they be – work in and through me. I am born to serve Thee, to be Thine, to be Thy instrument. Let me be Thy blind instrument. I ask not to see – I ask not to know – I ask simply to be used.

Appendix I

Meditations on Christian Doctrine

Hope in God – Creator

March 7, 1848

By John Henry Cardinal Newman

The Mission of My Life

1. God was all-complete, all-blessed in Himself; but it was His will to create a world for His glory. He is Almighty, and might have done all things Himself, but it has been His will to bring about His purposes by the beings He has created. We are all created to His glory – we are created to do His will. I am created to do something or to be something for which no one else is created; I have a place in God's counsels, in God's world, which no one else has; whether I be rich or poor, despised or esteemed by man, God knows me and calls me by my name.

2. God has created me to do Him some definite service; He has committed some work to me which He has not committed to another. I have my mission – I never may know it in this life, but I shall be told it in the next. Somehow I am necessary for His purposes, as necessary in my place as an archangel in his – if, indeed, I fail, He can raise another, as He could make the stones children of Abraham. Yet I have a part in this great work; I am a link in a chain, a bond of connection between persons. He has not created me for naught. I shall do good, I shall do His work; I shall be an angel of peace, a preacher of truth in my own place, while not intending it, if I do but keep His commandments and serve Him in my calling.

3. Therefore I will trust Him. Whatever, wherever I am, I can never be thrown away. If I am in sickness, my sickness may serve Him, in perplexity, my perplexity may serve Him; if I am in sorrow, my sorrow may serve Him. My sickness, or perplexity, or sorrow may be necessary causes of some great end, which is quite beyond us. He does nothing in vain; He may prolong my life, He may shorten it; He knows what He is about. He may take away my friends, He may throw me among strangers, He may make me feel desolate, make my spirits sink, hide the future from me – still He knows what He is about. *O Adonai*, O Ruler of Israel, Thou that guidest Joseph like a flock, *O Emmanuel, O Sapientia*, I give myself to Thee. I trust Thee wholly. Thou are wiser than I – more loving to me than I myself. Deign to fulfill Thy high purposes in me whatever they be – work in and through me. I am born to serve Thee, to be Thine, to be Thy instrument. Let me be Thy blind instrument. I ask not to see – I ask not to know – I ask simply to be used.

Work Cited

Armbruster, Jeffrey T., *Some Practical Lessons in Leadership – Observations from Daily Life*, Createspace, 2010.

Benedict XVI, *Porta Fidei*, an Apostolic Letter, *Libreria editrice Vaticana*, 2011.

Bolman, Lee G., and Deal, Terrence E., *Leading with Soul*, Josey-Bass, Inc. Publishers, 2002.

Bennis, Warren, *Managing People is Like Herding Cats*, Executive Excellence Publishing, 1997.

Cashman, Kevin, *Leadership from the Inside Out*, Executive Excellence Publishing, 1998.

Catechism of the Catholic Church, Doubleday, 1995.

Chuang Tzu, *The Inner Law*, in *The Way of Chuang Tzu* by Thomas Merton, New Directions, 2010 (Second Edition).

Covey, Stephen R., *The 7 Habits of Highly Effective People*, Simon & Schuster, 1989.

Dalai Lama, *Ethics for the New Millennium*, Riverhead Books, 2001.

Eurobarometer Poll, *Religion in Europe*, 2010.

Francis I, *Apostolic Exhortation – Evangelii Gaudium (The Joy of the Gospel)*, The Dynamic Catholic Institute with permission from the Vatican Press, 2014.

Francis I, *Bull of Indiction of the Extraordinary Jubilee Year of Mercy*, Vatican Press, 2015.

Ignatius of Loyola, *The Spiritual Exercises of St. Ignatius of Loyola*, Translated from the Autograph by Father Elder Mullan, S. J., P.J. Kennedy & Sons, 1914.

Hamlin, Rick, *A Faith Lesson from Mother Teresa*, Guidepost Magazine, May 17, 2012.

John Paul II, *Vita Consecrata (The Consecrated Life)*, Apostolic Exhortation, Libreria Editrice Vaticana, 1996

Kelly, Matthew, *Perfectly Yourself: 9 Lessons for Enduring Happiness*, Ballantine Books, 2008.

Kelly, Matthew, *The Seven Levels of Intimacy: The Art of Loving and the Joy of Being Loved*, Fireside Catholic Publishing, 2007.

Kreeft, Peter, *Making Choices – Finding Black and White in a World of Grays, Practical Wisdom for Everyday Moral Decisions*, Servant Books, 1990.

Kreeft, Peter, *How to Win the Culture War – A Christian Battle Plan for a Society in Crisis*, InterVarsity Press, 2002.

Kreeft, Peter, *The God Who Loves You*, Ignatius Press, 2004.

Kreeft, Peter, *Jesus Shock*, St. Augustine's Press, 2008.

Kun, Jeanne, editor, *Love Songs – Wisdom from Saint Bernard of Clairveaux*, The Word Among Us Press, 2001.

Lewis, C. S., *Screwtape Letters*, Harper Collins Publishers, Inc., 1942.

Lowney, Chris, *Heroic Leadership: Best Practices from a 450-Year-Old Company That Changed the World*, Loyola Press, 2005.

Manz, Charles C., *The Leadership Wisdom of Jesus*, Barrett-Koehler Publishers, Inc., 1998.

Merton, Thomas, *Disputed Questions*, Harvest Books, 1985.

Newman, John Henry, *The Mission of My Life, in Meditations on Christian Doctrine, Hope in God – Creator, March 7, 1848.*

Newman, John Henry, *God's Will the End of Life, from Discourses Addressed to Mixed Congregations*, 1849, in Daniel M. O'Connell, *Favorite Newman Sermons*, The America Press, 2nd ed., 1940, pp. 177-178.

Newman, John Henry, *The Three Offices of Christ in the Newman Reader – Works of John Henry Newman, Sermon 5*, The National Institute for Newman Studies, 2007.

Nouwen, Henri J. M., *Can you Drink the Cup?*, Ave Maria Press, 1996.

Pascal, Blaise, *Pensées*, (Translated by A.J. Krailsheimer), Penguin Classics, 1995.

Pascal, Blaise, *The Physical Treatises of Pascal: The Equilibrium of Liquids and Weight of the Mass of the Air (1653)*, Columbia University Press, 1937.

Patterson, Kerry; Grenny, Joseph; McMillan, Ron; and Switzler, Al, *Crucial Conversations*, McGraw-Hill, 2002.

Pew Form on Religion and Public Life, *U.S. Religious Knowledge Survey*, 2010.

Pisegna, Cedric, *You Can Change*, JC Productions, 2010.

Radcliff, Timothy, OP, *Taking the Plunge, Living Baptism and Confirmation*, Bloomsbury Publishing, 2012.

Rohr, Richard, *The Naked Now—Learning to see as the Mystics See*, The Crossroad Publishing Company, 2009.

Saint John Damascene, *Exposition of the Orthodox Faith - De Fide Orthodoxa*, Translated by Rev. S. D. F. Salmond, Christian Literature Publishing Company, 1886.

Sayers, Dorothy L., *Creed or Chaos?*, Sophia Institute Press, 1949.

Sri, Edward, and Martin, Curtis, *The Real Story—Understanding the Big Picture of the Bible*, The Dynamic Catholic Institute, 2012.

Staub, Robert E., *The Seven Acts of Courage*, Executive Excellence Publishing, 1999.

The Divine Office, Christian Prayer–The Liturgy of the Hours, Catholic Book Publishing Corporation, 1976.

The Word Among Us, A Catholic Devotional Magazine based on the Daily Mass Readings.

Thompson, Phillip M., *Returning to Reality—Thomas Merton's Wisdom for a Technological World*, Wipf & Stock Publishers, 2012.

U.S. Conference of Catholic Bishops, *To Be a Christian Steward – A Pastoral Letter on Stewardship*, 2013.

Williams, Thomas D., *Spiritual Progress*, Hachette Book Group, 2007.

Jeff Armbruster was born into a Roman Catholic family and has been active in church activities his entire life, including being a lector and an Extraordinary Minister of Holy Communion. He has been involved in pastoral planning, Christ Renews His Parish, and teaching adult education courses. Jeff, and his wife Laurel, together taught high school CCD and are a sponsor couple, having prepared 25 couples for marriage thus far. Over the years he has trained parish ministry leaders on teamwork concepts, and has facilitated in-depth internal assessment processes for two religious orders. Jeff has given spiritual talks at many Catholic and non-Catholic churches across Georgia and South Carolina. He is a member of the Advisory Committee to Catholic Charities Atlanta and is a founding member of the Steering Committee for Catholic Charities Atlanta's Leadership Class. Jeff has mentored a member of each class during the program's five-year existence.

Professionally, Jeff is Senior Consultant, Armbruster & Associates, LLC, although now mostly retired. For the past fourteen years, he has provided customized training, coaching, and consulting services to a wide range of clients, particularly in the areas of principle-centered leadership, emotional intelligence, teamwork effectiveness, and one-on-one executive coaching.

Jeff retired from the U.S. Geological Survey in 2001, after more than 37 years of public service. During his career with USGS, he spent 15 years working in the field of hydrology (he has both a BS and MS in Civil Engineering) and 20 years managing scientific research programs. During his final 2 years, he was a member of the USGS's Executive Leadership Team and served as one of the agency Director's senior policy advisors.

Jeff lives in Norcross, Georgia, with his wife and best friend, Laurel. They have two children, both married, and 3 grandchildren, so far! In his leisure time, he enjoys reading, traveling, woodworking, writing, and playing golf.

Notes

Notes

Made in the USA
Columbia, SC
23 July 2017